Blacks and Science
Volume Three

Blacks and Science Volume Three

*African American
Contributions to
Science and Technology*

BY

Robin Walker

REKLAW EDUCATION LTD
London (U.K.)

First published as an e-book in 2012 by Reklaw Education

ISBN-13: 978-1489518309

ISBN-10: 1489518304

CONTENTS

PREFACE

While browsing the internet, I came across an article that mentioned the following information: 'Thomas Jennings was the first African American to receive a patent, on March 3, 1821 (U.S. patent 3306x). Thomas Jennings' patent was for a dry-cleaning process called "dry scouring".'

While reading this, a number of thoughts came to me. An African American inventor? In 1821? Is this an exception or are there other examples?

After doing more research, I can now pose the question: Did YOU know that a camera invented by a Black astrophysicist was used during the Apollo 16 space mission to collect ultraviolet images photographed from the moon?

In fact did you know any of the following facts?

An early eighteenth century Virginia slave developed effective treatments against skin and venereal disease. In fact: 'His work was so outstanding that in 1729 the Virginia Legislature bought him from his owner, thus freeing him from slavery, to practice medicine exclusively'

Astronomical works by a late eighteenth century Black mathematician and astronomer were widely read and 'became a household staple in early America along with the Bible'

A nineteenth century African American blacksmith patented an invention described as 'the most important single invention in the whole history of whaling'

A nineteenth century inventor of Black South American heritage created such a revolution in the shoe industry, that it was said of him: 'What Edison is to artificial lighting, [he] is to footwear'

By 1913, African Americans held around 1,000 patents for various inventions in household goods, industrial machinery, transportation, electricity and chemical compounds

A Black physicist extended the Quantum Theory in the 1920s

Henry Ford described a Black botanist in the 1930s as 'the greatest living scientist'

Another Black chemist invented synthetic cortisone, an effective treatment for rheumatoid arthritis that broke the monopoly that European chemists had on the production of sterols

Twelve Black scientists and mathematicians worked on the Manhattan Project, i.e. the American nuclear bomb project, during World War II

A Black surgeon headed the blood bank system of the US and the UK during World War II

The research of a Black physicist and inventor of the 1960s may hold a key to addressing the main concerns of our times--dwindling sources of useable energy, rising energy costs, and increasing demand for energy

For too many people, it may be the first time that they had ever encountered such information. This is unfortunate. I believe that African and African Diasporan science history is a subject that has had too little attention paid to it. Some important writers have ventured into the field; Professor Ivan Van Sertima and his team, Mr J. A. Rogers, Mr Samuel Kennedy Yeboah, Dr Louis Haber, and Mr Hunter Havelin Adams III. My work synthesises and updates their findings. I also present the data in an easy to digest, bite-size way.

This book is one of three that introduces African and African Diasporan contributions to science and technology. The other two in the series concern Ancient Egypt, and sub Saharan Africa. This book began life as an e-book entitled *African American Contributions to Science and Technology.*

It is a general introduction to the role played by the African Americans in the evolution of the Space Sciences, Invention, Mathematics & Physics, Chemistry, Biology, Botany & Zoology, and Medicine & Surgery. I also present a useful commentary on *Theo's Story,* a popular tale that asks the reader to imagine life without the technological contributions of the African American inventors. I finally present excerpts from Henry E. Baker's classic 1913 text *The Colored Inventor.*

Read and enjoy

Robin Walker 2013

INTRODUCTION: IN THE SPACE SCIENCES

Dr George Carruthers

Dr George Carruthers (b. 1939) is an important contributor to the growing multi-disciplinary field of the space sciences. He designed the Far Ultraviolet Camera/Spectrograph carried by the Apollo 16 team to the moon. Because of the ultraviolet photographs of the earth taken from the moon by this device, one writer considers this the most significant single contribution in recent years to our knowledge of the world's physical structure. Another of Carruthers' devices captured an ultraviolet image of Halley's Comet in 1986.

Born in Ohio and the son of a civil engineer, the young Carruthers was a curious child who liked physics and enjoyed visiting museums and libraries. After visiting the Adler Planetarium, he became interested in astronomy, rocket construction and science fiction. He built his first telescope aged 10. He participated in science fairs during his school days and won three awards at those fairs.

Entering the College of Engineering at the University of Illinois, he achieved Bachelor's, Master's and PhD qualifications in aeronautical and

Figure 1. Dr George Carruthers (b. 1939).

Figure 2. Dr George Carruthers seen here with his camera/spectrograph.

astronomical engineering. His 1964 doctorate thesis concerned experimental investigations of atomic nitrogen recombination.

As a research physicist, he wrote two highly regarded papers which established his reputation as a formidable astrophysicist--*An Upper Limit on the Concentration of Molecular Hydrogen in Inter-stellar Space* and *Far Ultraviolet Spectroscopy and Photometry of some Early Type Stars.* Spectroscopy is the study of the relationship between matter and radiation. Photometry is about measuring the intensity of light coming from a light source such as a star. Carruthers would go on to write or co-write 63 important scientific papers for major journals and collections. He also received a 1969 patent for an 'Image Converter for Detecting Electromagnetic Radiation Especially in Short Wave Lengths.'

Perhaps his crowing achievement is his camera/spectrograph used by the Apollo 16 space mission. It was a semi automatic instrument that combined a camera with a spectrograph, with an electron intensifier. Carried to the moon in mid May 1972, the device took ultraviolet photographs of the lunar sky. It took photographs of the earth and selected celestial bodies. Thus for the first time, space explorers were able to record and study planetary and other astronomical data from the moon. Also in 1972 Dr Carruthers was awarded the Exceptional Achievement Scientific Award Medal from NASA (i.e. National Aeronautics and Space Administration).

In an essay, *Space Astronomy in the Shuttle Era,* Carruthers explains: 'The far ultraviolet ... is of great importance to the astronomer because it allows the detection and measurement of common elements (hydrogen, oxygen, nitrogen, carbon, and many others) in their cool, unexcited position ("Ground state" of the atom or molecule) a task which is difficult or impossible in the ground-accessible wavelength range. This allows more accurate measurements of the compositions of interstellar gas, planetary atmospheres, etc. The ultraviolet also conveys important information on solid particles ("dust") in interstellar space and elsewhere, and provides for much more accurate measurements of the energy outputs of very hot stars.'

On 12 February 2009, Dr Carruthers was honoured as a Distinguished Lecturer at the Office of Naval Research for his achievements in the field of space science. He is also a member of the American Astronomical Society, the American Geophysical Union, the American Institute of Aeronautics and Astronautics, and the American Association for the Advancement of Science.

African Americans at NASA

Other African American scientists and engineers have worked for NASA (i.e. National Aeronautics and Space Administration). Like Dr Carruthers, some of these have also made science history.

Dr 'Guy' Bluford (b. 1942), is an engineer, retired Colonel from the United States Air Force, but most importantly, a former NASA astronaut.

Figure 3. Dr 'Guy' Bluford (b. 1942), the first African American in space.

The first African American in space, Bluford participated in the 1983 mission STS-8, as a crew member of the Space Shuttle Challenger. He participated in four Space Shuttle flights between 1983 and 1992. His 1978 PhD from the Air Force Institute of Technology was in aerospace engineering with a minor in laser physics. More recently, he was inducted into the International Space Hall of Fame in 1997 and the United States Astronaut Hall of Fame in 2010.

Dr Christine Darden (b. 1942) was an aerospace engineer in the High Speed Aerodynamics Division at NASA's Langley Research Center at Hampton, Virginia. She was the leading NASA researcher in supersonic and hypersonic boom. In her own words: "[W]hen we fly above the speed of sound a shock wave is sent to the ground causing what is termed a sonic boom. These booms can be quite loud and devastating to people, animals, windows, and certain structures. In fact, supersonic flight over the U.S. is banned, for that reason. Even the Concorde cannot fly supersonically until it's over the Atlantic Ocean." Through designing wind tunnels and models of aircraft, her research aimed to reduce the sound of aircraft re entering the atmosphere. By manipulating the shapes of the craft and their wings, boom can be reduced. Her Bachelor's and Master's degrees were in Mathematics. Her PhD was in mechanical engineering from George Washington University. She has received several NASA Outstanding Performance and Achievement Awards, and also a Women in Engineering Lifetime Achievement Award.

Professor Isaac Gillam IV was at one time the Director of Dryden's Flight Research Center at Edwards Air Force Base in California from 1977 until 1981. Responsible for 1,000 space personnel, Gillam had the ultimate role in getting the Space Shuttle airborne. He oversaw the transportation of the shuttle to its launching pad at Cape Kennedy in Florida, to its safe flight into the heavens and to its safe landing in the Mojave Desert. He qualified in space science and engineering and became Assistant Professor of Air Science at Tennessee University. Ultimately, he received NASA's highest award, the Distinguished Service Medal, for his work on the Launch Vehicle Program.

Colonel Frederick Gregory (b. 1941) had a background as a test pilot for the U.S. Air Force and became an astronaut in 1978. Having flown over 40 different aircraft, he was involved with aircraft and simulation evaluation for both the Air Force and NASA. It was Gregory who flew the craft that field-tested the computer driven ground-based microwave landing system. Designed to eliminate human error in landing a craft, this system used

Figure 4. Professor Mae Carol Jemison (b. 1956), the first Black woman in space.

microwaves sent from the earth to the aircraft to control the landing. Gregory has also designed and redesigned cockpits for commercial aircraft and for the Space Shuttle. At the peak of his career in 2005, he became NASA's Acting Administrator.

Professor Mae Carol Jemison (b. 1956) had a background as a medical doctor. Having joined NASA as an astronaut, she became the first Black woman to travel in space. She went into orbit aboard the Space Shuttle Endeavour on 12 September 1992. After leaving NASA in 1993, she formed a company researching the application of technology to daily life. She appeared on television several times, even appearing in an episode of *Star Trek: The Next Generation*. She holds many honorary doctorates in science and engineering.

Dr Robert Shurney (d. 2007) was an aeronautical engineer and physicist. Working at the Marshall Space Flight Center, he designed and tested the commodes used aboard the Skylab. Moreover, he designed the tires used on the moon buggy FALCON for the Apollo 15 mission in 1972.

Having seen that African American scientists and engineers played important roles in the evolution of the Space Age, the key question I address in this book is: *Did these scientists and engineers come out of nowhere or is there a history to this?*

CHAPTER ONE: EARLY AFRICAN AMERICAN PIONEERS OF SCIENCE

The Pioneers

The earliest African Americans to contribute to scientific and technological endeavour were those who were held in bondage by European Americans.

Hunter Havelin Adams III, citing the research of Robert Hayden and Jacqueline Harris, tells the story of five such eighteenth century pioneers: 'Primus, a slave from Connecticut, helped his owner in surgery and in the general practice of medicine. When the doctor died, Primus took over his owner's practice. He was so successful throughout the country that even his former owner's white patients did not object to being treated by him. Papin, a Virginia slave, developed extremely effective treatments against skin and venereal disease. His work was so outstanding that in 1729 the Virginia Legislature bought him from his owner, thus freeing him from slavery, to practice medicine exclusively. In 1733 another Virginia slave was freed by the state and given a pension for life following his discovery of cures for scurvy and distemper. In 1[7]72, a slave named Caesar had gained such a reputation for his use of roots and herbs to cure poisoning, even rattlesnake bites, that the State of North Carolina purchased his freedom and gave him a pension of $500 a year for life ... In 1721 Onesimus described to his owner, Mather, the process of inoculation for the treatment of smallpox he received in Africa. Enthusiastically, Mather contacted ten other doctors in Boston and told them about the practice of deliberately infecting healthy persons with smallpox as a way to make the body immune to a severe attack of smallpox. One of them, Dr. Boylston, after successfully treating his son and two of his slaves, inoculated 241 people and only six of that group caught smallpox.'

There were other great pioneers during this period. James Derham (c.1757-1802) is thought to have been the first African American to formally practice medicine in the United States. Born into captivity in Philadelphia, Pennsylvania, he was owned by several doctors. However, one of his enslavers, the physician Dr Robert Love, encouraged him to go into medicine. By working as a nurse, Derham purchased his freedom by 1783. He opened a medical practice by the age of 26. His annual earnings

Figure 5. James Derham (c.1757-1802), the first African American to formally practice medicine.

were astounding! He earned in excess of $3,000. Derham met with Dr Benjamin Rush, considered the father of American medicine. Rush was so stunned by Derham that he encouraged him to move to Philadelphia. There he became an expert in throat diseases. He also became an expert in the relationship between climate and disease.

Benjamin Banneker

Benjamin Banneker (1731-1806) was the greatest of the early African American scientists. He was a mathematician, astronomer, clock maker, surveyor and author. He was also a land owner and gentleman farmer. Unlike the vast majority of African Americans at this time, he was born a free man. No one seems to be sure of how he achieved this status and the various theories advanced by historians are all unsatisfactory.

Which ever be the case, the young Banneker studied at a Quaker school where he excelled in mathematics. Initially he became fascinated by timepieces, but at a later date, he became interested in astronomy. Since some writers claim a Dogon ancestry for Banneker's father, this interest in astronomy may possibly have some link to the young Banneker's Dogon heritage.

In 1753 Banneker designed and built a wooden clock inspired by a pocket watch that a merchant or trader had given to him. Before making the clock, Banneker read an old journal from London which contained a picture of a

Figure 6. Benjamin Banneker (1731-1806), the greatest of the early African American scientists.

clock. He also read a book on geometry. He even read Isaac Newton's classic *Philosophiæ Naturalis Principia Mathematica.* Banneker's completed clock kept good time, striking on the hour, every hour, for 40 years.

His mathematical and astronomical knowledge led to his controversial prediction of a solar eclipse on 14 April 1789. What was controversial was that Banneker's prediction was based on correcting errors he discovered in the works of published astronomers and mathematicians, Leadbetter and Ferguson. Commenting on Fergusson's *Astronomy,* Banneker wrote: 'It appears to me that the wisest men may at times be in error; for instance, Dr. Fergusson informs us that, when the sun is within 12° of either node at the time of full, the moon will be eclipsed; but I find that, according to his method of projecting a lunar eclipse, there will be none by the above elements, and yet the sun is within 11° 46' 11" of the moon's ascending node. But the moon, being in her apogee, prevents the appearance of this eclipse.'

Having read Leadbetter's *Lunar Tables,* Banneker wrote: 'Errors that ought to be corrected in my astronomical tables are these: 2d vol. Leadbetter, p. 204, when anomaly is 4s 30° the equation 3° 30' 4" ought to have been 3° 28' 41".'

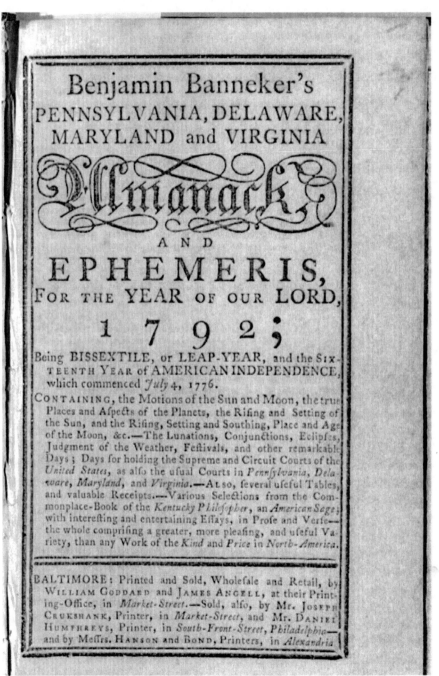

Figure 7. Benjamin Banneker's 1792 *Pennsylvania, Delaware, Maryland and Virginia Almanack and Ephemeris.*

In February 1791 Major Andrew Ellicott hired Banneker to assist him in the initial survey of the boundaries of the 100 square mile district that Maryland and Virginia would cede to the federal government of the United States. This district was to become the location of the soon to be built city of Washington.

Banneker's activities consisted of making astronomical observations at Jones Point in Alexandria, Virginia, to ascertain the location of the starting point for the survey. He also maintained a clock that he used to relate points on the surface of the Earth to the positions of the stars at specific times. Following this assignment, Banneker returned home to the village of Ellicott's Mill and set to work on more astronomical research.

He wrote up his astronomical calculations in a series of almanacs that appeared in a number of editions. These documents contained his predicted solar and lunar eclipses and their subsequent revisions. These were printed and sold in six cities in four American states for the years 1792 through 1797. Other almanacs were produced up the year 1802. He also kept a series of journals that contained his astronomical observations. He also kept a diary. The notebooks contained mathematical calculations and puzzles.

The title page of an edition of Banneker's 1792 *Pennsylvania, Delaware, Maryland and Virginia Almanack and Ephemeris* stated that the publication contained: '[T]he Motions of the Sun and Moon, the true Places and Aspects of the Planets, the Rising and Setting of the Sun, and the Rising, Setting and Southing, Place and Age of the Moon, &c.--The Lunations, Conjunctions, Eclipses, Judgment of the Weather, Festivals, and other remarkable Days; Days for holding the Supreme and Circuit Courts of the United States, as also the usual Courts in Pennsylvania, Delaware, Maryland, and Virginia.--ALSO, several useful Tables, and valuable Receipts.--Various Selections from the Commonplace-Book of the Kentucky Philosopher, an American Sage; with interesting and entertaining Essays, in Prose and Verse--the whole comprising a greater, more pleasing, and useful Variety, than any Work of the Kind and Price in North-America.'

The 1792 almanac included the times for the rising and setting of the sun and moon, weather forecasts, dates for yearly feasts, a tide table for Chesapeake Bay, and home treatments for illnesses. His 1793 almanac included letters sent between himself and Thomas Jefferson.

Supported by the Ellicott family and promoted relentlessly by the Society for the Promotion of the Abolition of Slavery of Maryland and of Pennsylvania, the early editions of the almanacs achieved commercial

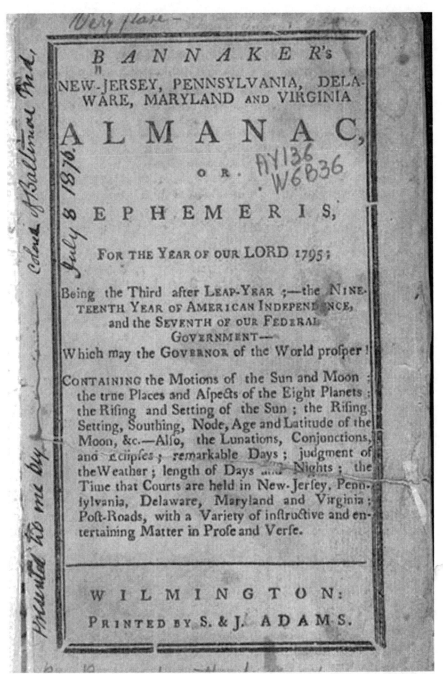

Figure 8. Benjamin Banneker's 1795 *New Jersey, Pennsylvania, Delaware, Maryland and Virginia Almanac or Ephemeris.*

success. According to Dr Louis Haber whose excellent *Black Pioneers of Science and Invention* inspired this book, the almanacs were widely read and 'became a household staple in early America along with the Bible.'

In Britain, the politicians Pitt, Fox and Wilberforce were impressed. The House of Commons issued a version of Banneker's almanac as evidence of the mental cultivation of the Black race.

CHAPTER TWO: AFRICAN AMERICAN PIONEERS IN INVENTION

Introducing the Black Pioneers of Invention

By 1913, scholars estimate that African Americans held around 1,000 patents for various inventions in household goods, industrial machinery, transportation, electricity and chemical compounds. Amongst these pioneers were:

Bailery, L. C. inventor of a folding bed, patent number 629,286 received 18 July 1899

Beard, A. J. inventor of a car coupler, patent number 594,059 received 23 November 1897

Brooks, C. B. inventor of a street sweeper, patent number 556,711 received 17 March 1896

Burr, J. A. inventor of a lawn mower, patent number 624,749 received 9 May 1899

Burridge, L. S. inventor of a type writing machine, patent number 316,386 received 7 April 1895

Butler, R. A. inventor of a train alarm, patent number 584,540 received 15 June 1897

Campbell, W. S. inventor of a self-setting animal trap, patent number 246,349 received 30 August 1881

Ferrell, F. J. inventor of a set of valves for steam engines, patent number 428,671 received 25 May 1890

Grant, G. F. inventor of a golf tee, patent number 638,920 received 12 December 1899

Headen, M. inventor of a foot power hammer, patent number 350,363 received 5 October 1886

Lee, J. inventor of a bread crumbling machine, patent number 540,553 received 4 June 1895

Marshall, T. J. inventor of a fire extinguisher, patent number 125,063 received 26 May 1872

Miles, A. inventor of an elevator, patent number 371,207 received 11 October 1887

Murray, G. W. inventor of a fertilizer distributer, patent number 520,889 received 5 June 1894

Pickering, J. F. inventor of an air ship, patent number 643,975 received 20 February 1900

Purvis, W. B. inventor of a paper bag machine, patent number 420,099 received 28 January 1890

Sampson, G. T. inventor of a clothes drier, patent number 476,416 received 7 June 1896

Stanard, J. inventor of a refrigerator, patent number 455,891 received 14 July 1891

Winters, J. R. inventor of a fire escape ladder, patent number 203,517 received 7 May 1878

It must be stated however, that there is a difference between inventing *A* 'folding bed' and inventing *THE* 'folding bed'. The prototypes for nearly all the non electronic devices that we use today are to be found in the technology of the ancient civilisations. It is reasonable to conclude therefore that many devices have actually been invented many times before at a variety of different times and in many different places around the world.

Another issue is that most African Americans before 1865 were enslaved. This meant they were legally unable to patent their discoveries since a patent was considered a contract between the United States government and a citizen. Enslaved Africans were not considered citizens of the United States and therefore could not own patents. In many such situations, their enslaver actually achieved the patent.

Robert Hayden, an authority whose research influenced a large part of this chapter, gives two examples of this: 'Jo Anderson, a slave on the plantation of Cyrus McCormick, is said to have made a major contribution to the McCormick grain harvester. Yet, he is only credited in the official records as being a handyman or helper to McCormick. In 1862, a slave owned by Jefferson Davis, President of the Confederacy, invented a

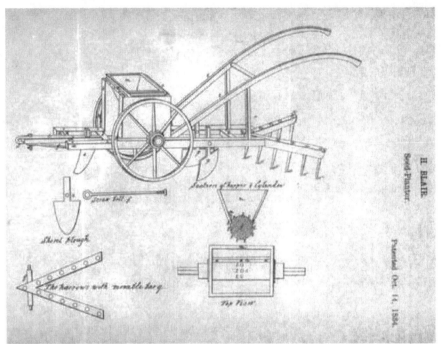

Figure 9. Patent of the Seed Planter invented by Henry Blair, received 14 October 1834.

propeller for ocean vessels. With a model of his invention the slave showed remarkable mechanical skill in wood and metal working. He was unable to get a patent on his propeller, but the merits of his invention were reported in many southern newspapers. The propeller was finally used in ships of the Confederate Navy.'

However, the 'free persons of colour,' unlike the relatively unmixed Blacks, were considered citizens of the United States and could therefore hold patents. These people were often of very mixed African and European ancestry. Society classified them quite differently to Blacks or Negroes. As an example, Henry Blair held a patent in 1834 for a seed planter. In 1836 he received a patent for a corn harvester. Another example was Norbert Rillieux. In 1846 he received an important patent that revolutionised the sugar manufacturing industry.

The rest of this chapter contains details of the more important Black inventors: Lewis Temple, Jan Matzeliger, Elijah McCoy, Granville Woods, Lewis Latimer, Garret Morgan, Frederick Jones, Otis Boykin and Dr Meredith Gourdine.

Lewis Temple

Figure 10. Lewis Temple (1800-1854). Inventor of the 'Temple's Toggle,' once considered the most impportant single invention in the entire history of whaling.

Lewis Temple (1800-1854) was a blacksmith and inventor whose discovery, according to an authority on whaling, 'was the most important single invention in the whole history of whaling. It resulted in the capture of a far greater proportion of whales that were struck than had before been possible.'

Born into bondage in Richmond, Virginia, Temple moved to the whaling village of New Bedford, Massachusetts in 1830.

In 1848 he invented a type of toggling harpoon that is sometimes called 'Temple's Toggle.' Manufactured for the New England whaling industry, Temple's device solved the problem that had bedevilled standard harpoons. Their barbed heads were no match for the power of the twisting and turning of a whale. Many whales broke free.

In response to this problem, Temple invented a moveable harpoon head. It toggled at right angles to the shaft and locked into the flesh of the whale. The effectiveness of the device led to it having almost universal use. In some parts of the Caribbean, it is still used today.

Jan Earnst Matzeliger

Jan Earnst Matzeliger (1852-1889) produced inventions that ultimately created the modern shoe industry. According to J. A. Rogers: 'What Edison is to artificial lighting, Matzeliger is to footwear. The great ... genius needs no monument. Almost every shoe worn by civilized men is his monument.'

Figure 11. Jan Earnst Matzeliger (1852-1889), the inventor who created the modern shoe industry.

Matzeliger was from Surinam in South America, born of Dutch and Afro-Surinamese parents. Aged 10 he worked in the government machine shops in his native Surinam showing aptitude for mechanics. Becoming a sailor and later a cobbler in the United States, Matzeliger became proficient in English. He also went to evening school and spent his meagre earnings on physics books and books on other subjects. As a cobbler, he operated a stitching machine working at the Harney-Brothers Shoe Factory in Lynn, Mass.

In the shoe industry, Matzeliger found that there were no machines at the time that could sew the uppers to the sole of the shoe. Inventors in Europe had produced sewing machines that could be used on shoe leather, but none could effectively last shoes (i.e. connect the upper and lower parts of the shoe). This had to be done by hand, thus creating the problem of bottlenecks which ultimately slowed down the production processes.

After much trial and error, Matzeliger produced the lasting machine, patent number 274,207 on 20 March 1883. The patented machine was his third attempt after constructing a model, then a full sized machine, which others attempted to buy for $1,500.

Matzeliger wrote the following information to the patent office to explain his device: 'My invention relates to the lasting of boots and shoes. The object of it is to perform by machinery and in a more expeditious and

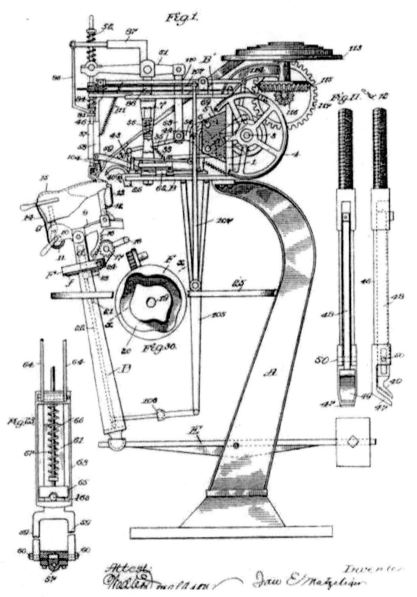

Figure 12. Patent of the Lasting Machine invented by Jan Earnst Matzeliger, number 274,207, received 20 March 1883.

economical manner the operations which have heretofore been performed by hand. Heretofore devices have been contrived for performing a part of the operation, such as holding the last in proper position and drawing the leather over the last, while the nailing was done by hand. In my machine, I perform all the operations by the machine, and automatically, requiring only the service of a boy or girl or other unskilled labor to attend the machine.'

According to the pioneering researcher on Black inventors, Henry E. Baker: 'Other machines had previously been made for performing a part of these operations, but Matzeliger's machine was the only one then known to the mechanical world that could simultaneously hold the last in place to receive the leather, move it forward step by step so that other co-acting parts might draw the leather over the heel, properly punch and grip the upper and draw it down over the last, plait the leather properly at the heel and toe, feed the nails to the driving point, hold them in position while being driven, and then discharge the completely soled shoe from the machine, everything being done automatically, and requiring less than a minute to complete a single shoe. This wonderful achievement marked the beginning of a distinct revolution in the art of making shoes by machinery. Matzeliger realized this, and attempted to capitalize it by organizing a stock company to market his invention;'

Having reduced the time of producing one shoe to one minute, eventually it became possible to produce 700 pairs of shoes in one day. This resulted in the costs of shoe production falling by one-half. Following this, Matzeliger formed the Union Lasting Machine Company with the backing of two investors. Other money men bought his patents and founded the Consolidated Lasting Machine Company. Matzeliger held shares in the company.

Henry E. Baker narrates the next part of the story: 'but his plans were frustrated through failing health and lack of business experience, and shortly thereafter, at the age of 36, he passed away. He had done his work, however, under the keen eye of the shrewd Yankees, and these were quick to see the immense commercial importance of the step he had accomplished. One of these bought the patent and all of the stock that he could find of the company organized by Matzeliger. This fortunate purchase laid the foundation for the organization of the United Shoe Machinery Company, the largest and richest corporation of the kind in the world ... Some idea may be had of the magnitude of this giant industry, which is thus shown to have grown directly out of the inventions of a young colored man, by recalling the fact that the corporation represents the

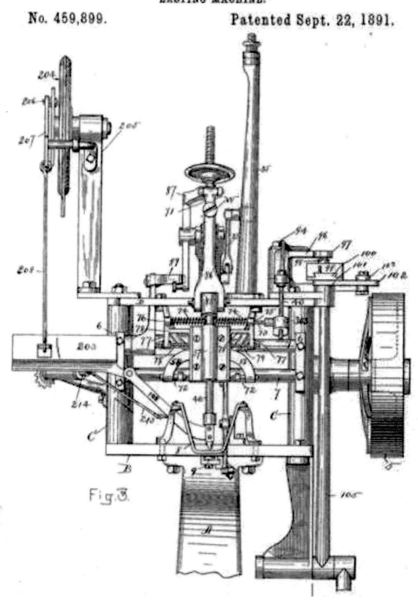

J. E. MATZELIGER, Dec'd.
G. W. MOULTON, EXECUTOR.
LASTING MACHINE.

No. 459,899.   Patented Sept. 22, 1891.

Fig. 3.

Figure 13. Patent of an improved Lasting Machine invented by Jan Earnst Matzeliger, number 459,899, received 22 September 1891.

consolidation of forty-one different smaller companies, that its factories cover twenty-one acres of ground, that it gives employment daily to 4,200 persons, that its working capital is quoted at $20,860,000, and that it controls more than 300 patents representing improvements in the machines it produces. From an article published in the Lynn (Mass.) *News,* of October 3, 1889, it appears that the United Shoe Machinery Company, above mentioned, established at Lynn a school, the only one of its kind in the world, where boys are taught exclusively to operate the Matzeliger type of machine; that a class of about 200 boys and young men are graduated from this school annually and sent out to various parts of the world to instruct others in the art of handling this machine.'

Matzeliger's other inventions included the mechanism for distributing tacks and nails, patented in 1888. Two years later, he received posthumous patents for the nailing machine and the tack separating and distributing mechanism. The following year, 1891, he received another posthumous patent for an improved lasting machine.

After his death, not only did the United Shoe Machinery Company of Boston buy these patents, they ultimately created a billion dollar industry out of them by 1955. According to J. A. Rogers: 'With this new invention, the United Shoe Manufacturing Company rapidly drove competitors out of the shoe business until, a few years later, it controlled 98 percent of the shoe machinery business.' Some Russian engineers after the Bolshevik Revolution wrote up and published Matzeliger's story in Russian.

Elijah McCoy

Elijah McCoy (1844-1929) was the 'Father of Lubrication.' It is said that when people of his time purchased engines, they would enquire whether it contained McCoy's lubricating cups. If it did then 'It's the real McCoy.'

McCoy was born in Canada. His parents were former slaves from the United States who escaped to Canada with the help of the Underground Railroad. They did, however, move back to the United States where they lived in Michigan.

The young McCoy attended grammar school in Michigan. In his early years, he was fascinated by machines and was often successful in fixing them. Leaving the country, he apprenticed as a mechanical engineer in Edinburgh, Scotland. Returning to the United States as a fully trained mechanical engineer, he found employment as a fireman for the Michigan Central Railroad. However, he was confronted with an engineering problem that he set about solving.

Figure 14. Elijah McCoy (1844-1929), the Father of Lubrication.

There was the problem of having to stop the trains periodically to oil the parts to reduce friction. As metal rubbed against metal in the movement of the train, the moving parts would become hot and then expand. This caused friction, which lead to metal joints becoming worn or even seizing up altogether. To prevent this, rail companies would have periods of downtime when they stopped the trains allowing the joints to cool. They would also lubricate the joints with oil.

In July 1872 McCoy patented his solution to this mechanical problem-- the first automatic lubricator. According to McCoy, his device 'provided for the continuous flow of oil on the gears and other moving parts of a machine in order to keep it lubricated properly and continuously and thereby do away with the necessity of shutting down the machine periodically.'

His discovery was applicable to steam engines and to steam cylinders. He improved the design in 1873 resulting in factories across the United States adopting McCoy's lubricating cups. He opened a factory in Detroit, Michigan called the Elijah McCoy Manufacturing Company to develop and market his patented lubricating devices. He received 25 patents for lubricators between 1873 and 1899.

In 1892 he applied the models to railway locomotives. According to Dr Haber, McCoy's system was used by 'all railroads in the West and on steamers on the Great Lakes.'

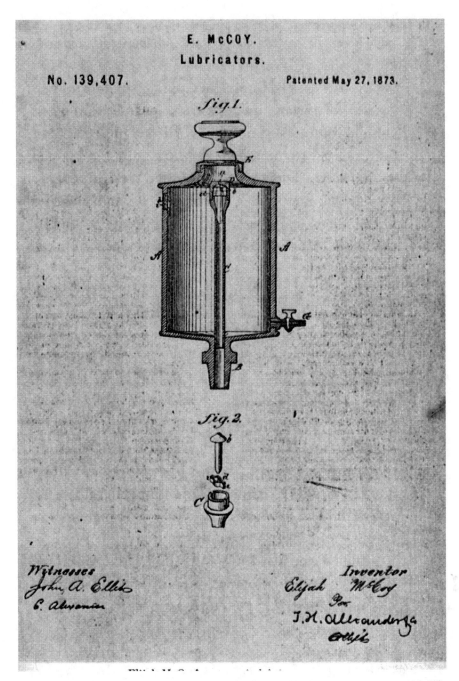

Figure 15. Patent of the Lubricator invented by Elijah McCoy number 139,407, received 27 May 1873.

In 1920 McCoy applied the same concept to air brakes. In total, Elijah McCoy held over 50 patents including an ironing table and a lawn sprinkler.

Granville T. Woods

Granville T. Woods (1856-1910) is sometimes called the 'Black Edison' due to his inventions in the field of electricity. He invented devices that improved electrical railway systems, improvements in telegraphy, telephones, automatic cut-offs for electrical circuits, and electric motor regulators. He sold his patents to American Bell Telephone, General Electric and Westinghouse Air Brake.

Due to having to work, the young Woods never completed school in his native Ohio. He did, however, work in a machine shop and thus had some mechanical experience. Later, he worked as a fireman and an engineer on the railways. Initially, he taught himself electricity from reading library books and borrowing books from friends and employers. Following this, he enrolled on a course in mechanical and electrical engineering.

By the year 1881, Woods had opening his own factory manufacturing equipment for the telephone, telegraph and electrical industries. He also became interested in the possibilities afforded by thermal power and steam engines.

In 1884 he received a patent for his invention of a steam boiler furnace. The following year, he invented a device that combined a telegraph with a telephone transmitter. From this device, Woods coined the word 'Telegraphony,' a combination of telegraph and telephone. The American Bell Telephone Company of Boston bought this device off him. In 1887 Woods invented railway telegraphy. His device could send messages between moving trains to reduce the possibility of railway collisions.

In 1890 he patented an egg incubator. In 1896 he patented a dimmer switch device which was safe and reduced electrical use by over 40 percent. In 1901 he invented the third rail which was in use in the New York Subways and elsewhere. In 1902, 1903 and 1905, he received a series of patents for devices that led to the automatic air brake.

Woods achieved a total of over 60 patents in electric railways, electrical control and distribution, telephone instruments, cut-offs for circuits, and electric motor regulators. His work attracted the attention of technical and scientific journals in the United States and elsewhere. Dr Haber says: 'Few inventors of any race have produced a larger number of appliances in the field of electricity.'

Figure 16. Granville T. Woods (1856-1910), the Black Edison.

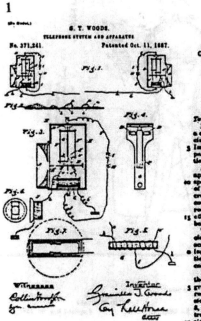

Figure 17. Patent of the Telephone System and Apparatus invented by Granville T. Woods number 371,241, received 11 October 1887.

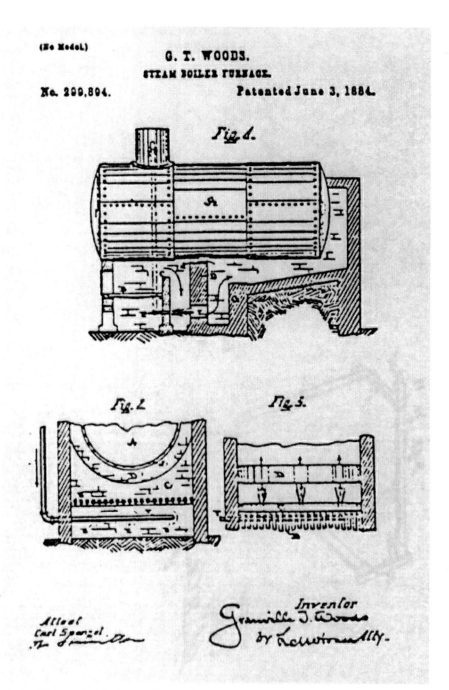

Figure 18. Patent of the Steam Boiler Furnace invented by Granville T. Woods number 299,894, received 3 June 1884.

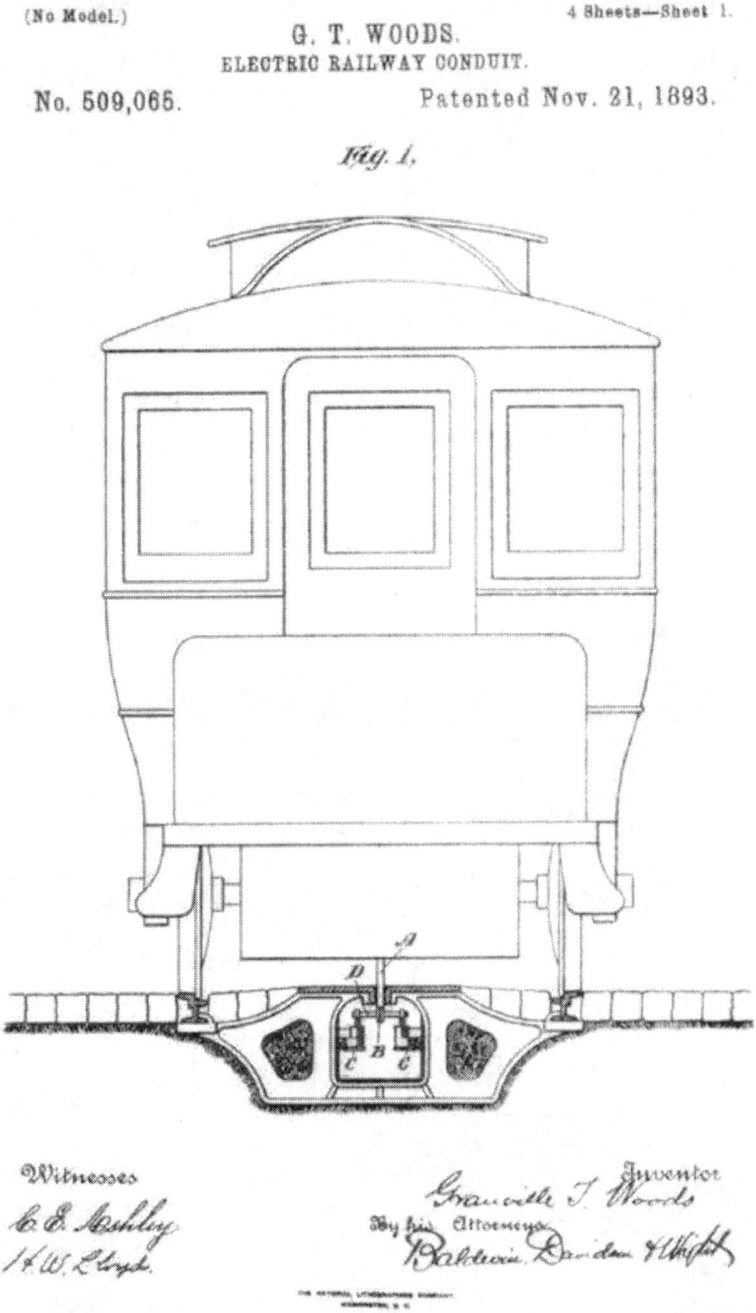

(No Model.)

4 Sheets—Sheet 1.

G. T. WOODS.
ELECTRIC RAILWAY CONDUIT.

No. 509,065.

Patented Nov. 21, 1893.

Fig. 1,

Figure 19. Patent of the Electric Railway Conduit invented by Granville T. Woods number 509,065, received 21 November 1893.

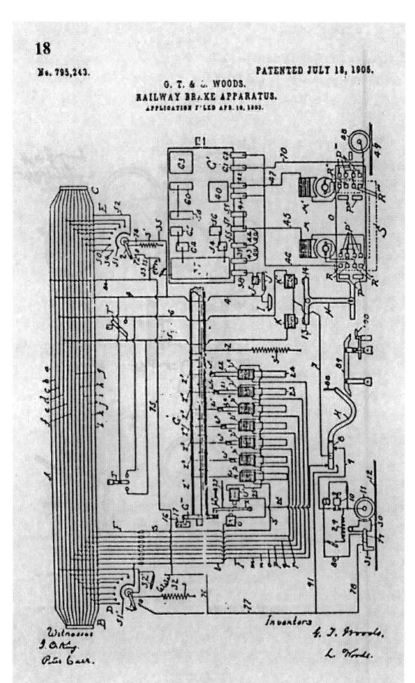

Figure 20. Patent of the Railway Brake Apparatus invented by Granville T. Woods number 795,243, received 18 July 1905.

Lewis Howard Latimer

Lewis Howard Latimer (1848-1928) was the distinguished inventor who one writer calls 'Bringer of the Light.' Outside of his specialist field of electricity, Latimer invented an apparatus for 'cooling and disinfecting,' a 'locking rack for hats, coats and umbrellas,' and a 'book support.' Ultimately he became the only Black member of the Edison Pioneers--the 28 brilliant scientists and inventors who worked with Thomas Edison. They formed their association in 1918.

Born in Mass., Latimer's schooling was interrupted aged ten when he had little option but to work to support his mother and siblings. Aged 16, he fought as part of the Naval Service during the Civil War. Following this, he became an office boy and later promoted to chief draughtsman, working for Crosby & Gould--a firm of patent solicitors. It was Latimer who prepared the drawings for Alexander Graham Bell's telephone patent of 1876.

In 1874 Latimer received a patent for a water closet for railroad cars, number 147,363, one of his first patents.

In 1880 he was hired as a draughtsman for Hiram Maxim, chief engineer for the United States Electric Light Company. During this period and inspired by Thomas Edison's breakthroughs in electricity, Latimer patented an electric light with a colleague called Joseph V. Nichols in 1881. Writing about this patent, Latimer and Nichols wrote: 'Our invention relates to

Figure 21. Lewis Howard Latimer (1848-1928), the Bringer of the Light.

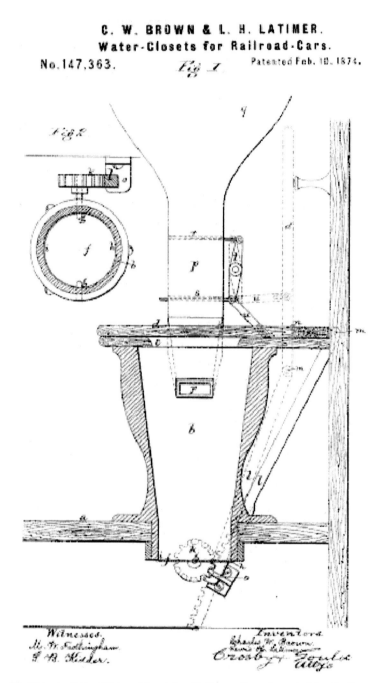

Figure 22. Patent of the Water Closet for Railway Cars invented by Latimer and Brown number 147,363, received 10 February 1874.

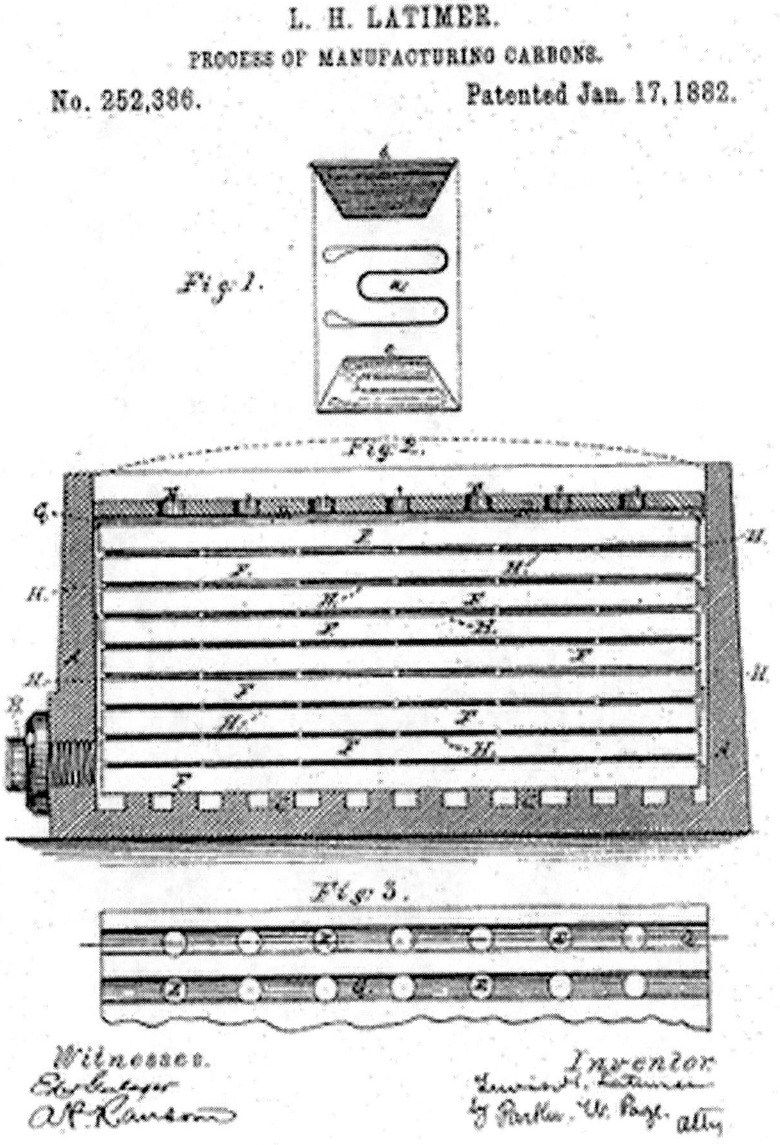

L. H. LATIMER.

PROCESS OF MANUFACTURING CARBONS.

No. 252,386.   Patented Jan. 17, 1882.

Figure 23. Patent of the Process of Manufacturing Carbons invented by Lewis Latimer number 252,386, received 17 January 1882.

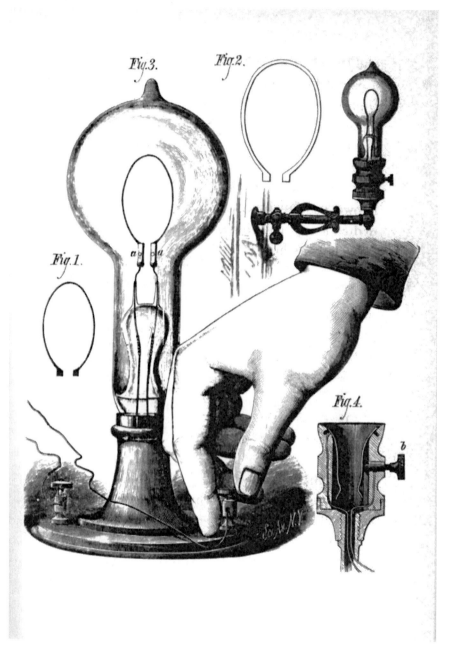

Figure 24. Page from Latimer's textbook, *Incandescent Electrical Lighting: A Practical Description of the Edison System* **(New York, Van Nostrand Company, 1890).**

electric lamps in which the light is produced by the incandescence of a continuous strip of carbon secured to metallic wires and enclosed in a hermetically sealed and thoroughly exhausted transparent receiver; and it relates more especially to the method of mounting that carbon or connecting them with the wires.'

In 1882 Latimer achieved his most celebrated patent of them all--a process of manufacturing carbons. Unlike the earlier bulbs of Edison, Latimer's discovery produced bulbs that not only lasted longer, but could be practically used in domestic and industrial settings. Latimer assigned this patent to his employer, the United States Electric Light Company.

Latimer also invented the globe support for electric lamps, patented that same year. Some of his electric lamp sockets were at one time on display in the Smithsonian Institute, Washington.

Latimer installed electric lighting in various buildings in New York City including the Equitable Building, and the Union League Club. He also installed electric lighting in Philadelphia and in Canada. Here, he learned French in order to give his orders to the Canadian workers. In autumn 1881 Latimer and his wife were sent to Britain. Latimer was given the mission of setting up an incandescent light department for the Maxim Weston Electric Light Company in London.

In 1884 Thomas Edison recruited Latimer for the engineering department of the Edison Electric Light Company, New York. Six years later, he transferred to the legal department. That year he wrote the standard work on electric lighting *Incandescent Electrical Lighting: A Practical Description of the Edison System* (New York, Van Nostrand Company, 1890) from which we extract the following: 'If the electric current can be forced through a substance that is a poor conductor, it will create a degree of heat in that substance which will be greater or less according to the quantity of electricity through it. Upon this principle of the heating effect of the electric current is based the operation of the incandescent lamp just described. While the copper and platinum wires readily conduct the current, a carbon filament offers a great deal of resistance to its passage and for this reason becomes very hot, in fact is raised to white heat or incandescence, which gives its name to the lamp.'

Garrett A. Morgan

Garrett A. Morgan (1877-1963) was a celebrated inventor best known for his creation of the breathing device, also known as the gas mask, used as a

Figure 25. Garrett A. Morgan (1877-1963).

key health and safety device by the police, fire departments and mining companies.

Originally from Tenn., he moved to Ohio. Morgan was totally self-educated. Initially, he worked as a machine adjuster. Later he set up a business selling and repairing sewing machines. In 1901 he invented a belt fastener for sewing machines. Following this, he owned a tailoring shop.

Somewhere around 1913, he discovered a chemical compound that straightened human hair. However, his most useful invention came a year later. He patented a breathing device which won the First Grand Prize at the Second International Exposition of Safety and Sanitation in New York City. His invention was used by Fire Departments all over the US. It was used by Police Departments and Mining Companies. Others versioned it creating the gas mask, used by the US Army during World War I. Morgan himself used the device to rescue trapped workers in 1916 and received a bravery medal from the City of Cleveland. However, Morgan faced the ugly face of racism. Yeboah reports: 'Orders began to pour into Cleveland as many municipalities purchased the Morgan inhalator. However, the orders soon stopped when the racial identity of the inventor became known.'

In this book, I have tried to keep the issue focused on the education and scientific achievements of the Black innovators. However, the role of

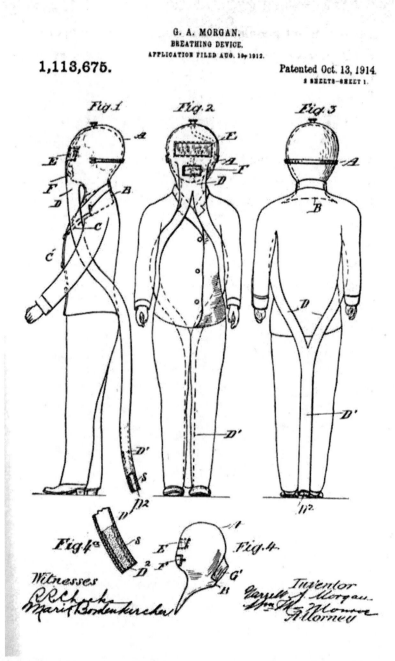

G. A. MORGAN.
BREATHING DEVICE.
APPLICATION FILED AUG. 19, 1912.

1,113,675.

Patented Oct. 13, 1914.
2 SHEETS-SHEET 1.

Figure 26. Patent of the Breathing Device invented by Garrett Morgan, number 1,113,675, received 13 October 1914.

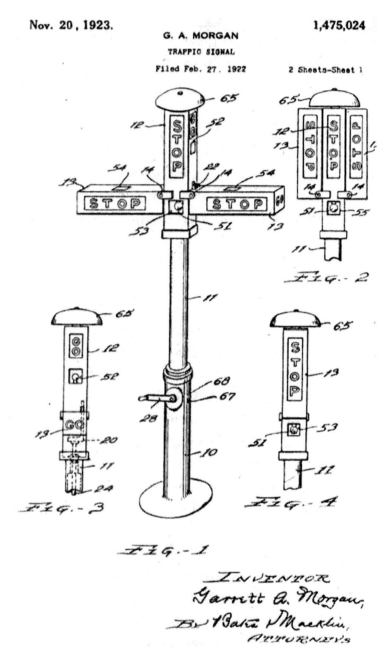

Figure 27. This is the controversial patent, number 1,475,024, which has caused much ink to flow.

racism cannot be ignored. It is on record how racism and segregation instituted by the European Americans blighted the lives, education or careers of Matzeliger, Bouchet, Turner, Just, Imes, Julian, etc. Nor were the incidents trivial, for instance in the case of Dr Julian, an arsonist attempted to burn down his home. Nor can we ignore the role of enslavement and other criminal activities often supported by the American government blight the lives, education and careers of Primus, Papin, Caesar, Onesimus, Derham, Anderson, Carver, etc. For example, the teenage Carver, while in Fort Scott, Kansas, witnessed a White mob drenching a Black man with oil and throwing him onto a bonfire.

Returning to Morgan, in 1923 he achieved his most controversial patent --number 1,475,024. This was a semaphore signal that controlled the flow of car traffic. Often wrongly described as the traffic lights, it can correctly be described as one of the predecessors to the traffic lights. As Dr Haber points out, Morgan in 1963 'was cited by the U.S. Government for inventing the first traffic signal.' Since other traffic signals existed before Morgan's device, the US Government may be wrong on this point. Perhaps instead they should have said ONE of the early traffic signals. However, even Morgan's critics concede that his device was an ingenious piece of invention.

Frederick McKinley Jones

Frederick McKinley Jones (1893-1961) was the inventor whose innovations in refrigeration revolutionised the food transport industry. Jones was an inventor, entrepreneur, winner of the National Medal of Technology, and inductee into the National Inventors Hall of Fame.

Orphaned as a boy, Jones found employment as an apprentice automobile mechanic and worked to build racing cars. He boosted his natural mechanical ability with independent reading and study. After serving in the US Army during World War I, he taught himself electronics and built a transmitter for his local town's new radio station. He also invented a device to combine sound with motion pictures. This attracted the attention of Joseph Numero of Minneapolis, who hired Jones in 1930 to improve the sound equipment made by his firm, Cinema Supplies Inc.

However, in the early 1930s, Jones devised a practical solution to a problem faced by a friend of his boss who was then working in the trucking industry. The trucker attempted to transport a consignment of poultry to a marketplace, but the ice melted before the trucker got there, thus spoiling

Figure 28. Frederick McKinley Jones (1893-1961), the inventor who revolutionised the food transport industry.

the poultry. Addressing this problem in around 1935, Jones designed a portable air-cooling unit for trucks carrying perishable food. He received a patent for it on 12 July 1940.

Numero sold his movie sound equipment business to RCA and formed a new company in partnership with Jones, the US Thermo Control Company which evolved into a $3 million business by 1949. Portable cooling units designed by Jones were especially important during World War II, preserving blood, medicine, and food for use at army hospitals and on open European battlefields. In short, Jones' inventions saved lives.

During his life, Jones received 61 patents. Forty were for refrigeration equipment, while others were for portable X-ray machines, sound equipment, and gasoline engines. He patented many of the special parts of his refrigeration equipment such as the self-starting gasoline engine that turned his cooling units on and off, the reverse cycling mechanism that produced heat or cold, and devices that controlled air temperature or moisture.

In 1944 Jones became the first African American to be elected into the American Society of Refrigeration Engineers. Even scientists and engineers that had college backgrounds were keen to work with him, a man with little formal education.

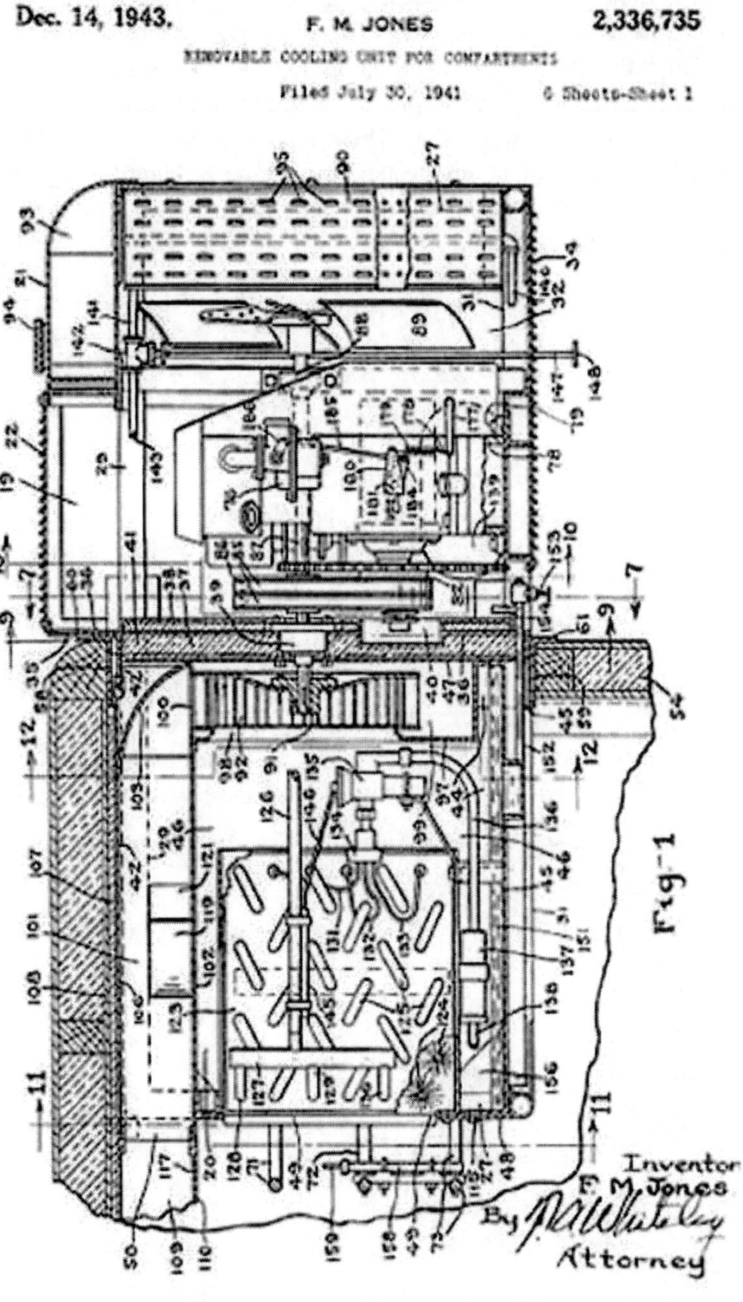

Dec. 14, 1943. F. M. JONES 2,336,735

REMOVABLE COOLING UNIT FOR COMPARTMENTS

Filed July 30, 1941 6 Sheets-Sheet 1

Figure 29. Patent of the Removable Cooling Unit for Compartments invented by Frederick McKinley Jones, number 2,336,735, received 14 December 1943.

In the 1950s he became a consultant to the US Department of Defence and the Bureau of Standards where he gave advice on refrigeration.

In 1991 the National Medal of Technology was awarded to Numero and Jones. President George Bush presented the awards posthumously to their widows at a ceremony in the White House Rose Garden. One writer, Samuel Kennedy Yeboah suggests: 'Today, there is hardly anyone in the West, and many parts of the world for that matter, whose life is unaffected by Jones' inventions.'

Otis Frank Boykin

Otis Frank Boykin (1920-1982) was an inventor and engineer specialising in electronic devices. His most celebrated invention was the control device for heart pacemakers.

The son of a carpenter, he attended the Booker T. Washington High School in Dallas, Texas, where he graduated in 1938. He attended Fisk University on a scholarship; he worked as a laboratory assistant at the nearby University's aerospace laboratory. He then moved to Chicago where he studied at the Illinois Institute of Technology, but only completed two years. Nevertheless, his talent was recognised by Dr Hal Fruth, an engineer and inventor with his own laboratory, who became his mentor. Ultimately the two men would collaborate on a number of research projects.

Boykin ultimately invented more than 25 electronic devices. One of his early inventions was an improved electrical resistor for use in computers,

Figure 30. Otis Frank Boykin (1920-1982), inventor of electronic devices.

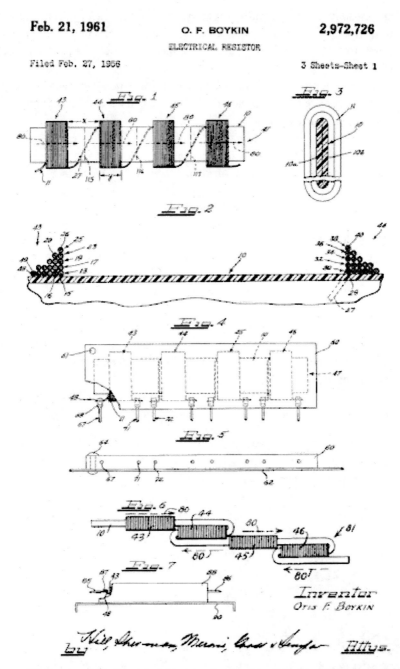

Feb. 21, 1961   O. F. BOYKIN   2,972,726
                          ELECTRICAL RESISTOR

Filed Feb. 27, 1956   3 Sheets-Sheet 1

Figure 31. Patent of the Electrical Resistor invented by Otis Frank Boykin, number 2,972,726, received 21 February 1961.

radios and televisions. He also invented an assortment of other electronic devices. One such invention was a variable resistor used in guided missiles. Another invention was the small component thick-film resistors for computers.

However, Boykin's most celebrated invention was a control unit for the artificial heart pacemaker. The device essentially uses electrical impulses to maintain a regular heartbeat.

From 1964 and into his later years, Boykin worked as a private research consultant for several American and French firms. At one time 37 of his products were manufactured in Paris and sold across Western Europe.

Meredith Charles Gourdine

Dr Meredith Charles Gourdine (1929-1998) was an engineer and physicist. His revolutionary work on electrogasdynamics is still of key importance. It has a great potential to address the main concerns of our times--dwindling sources of useable energy, rising energy costs, and increasing demand for energy.

Born in New Jersey, Gourdine graduated from Brooklyn Technical High School and studied physics at Cornell University. After earning his bachelor's degree in engineering in 1953, he became an officer in the United States Navy.

In 1960 he earned a doctorate in engineering from the California Institute of Technology working at the Jet Propulsion Laboratory from 1958 to

Figure 32. Dr Meredith Charles Gourdine (1929-1998), engineer and physicist, who addressed the key issue of dwindling sources of useable energy.

1960. After this, he worked for the aeronautical division of Curtiss-Wright Corporation where he became fascinated by an energy conversion method first decribed by European scientists in the eighteenth century. This process involved the interaction of charged particles with a moving gas stream which can produce very high voltage out of a low voltage originally generated. The problem, here, was that no one had produced any practical way to use this principle to generate enough electricity that could viably be used.

Dr Gourdine would eventually solve this problem by inventing electrogasdynamic systems and creating practical applications of the energy conversion process. Initially, he produced his own generator but failed to sell it to his then employer.

Instead, with an investment of $200,000 he founded his own firm--Gourdine Systems, Inc. From its original inception as a centre of research and development, Gourdine Systems evolved to apply electrogasdynamics to energy conversion and generation, air pollution control, printing, and finally paint-spraying systems.

For example, Dr Gourdine's techniques involved using pulverized low-grade coal and air in a combustion chamber to create cheap, transportable high voltage electricity. Other engineering techniques removed air pollution from urban areas, smoke from buildings, and fog from airport runways. His techniques ionised dust particles which were driven to a collection point by a stream of air.

In 1966 the US Department of the Interior, Office of Coal Research, awarded Dr Gourdine over $600,000 to perfect a model generator that used low-grade coal to generate 80,000 volts of electricity. The generator made no use of steam and had no moving parts.

Ultimately, Dr Gourdine was inducted into the Dayton, Ohio, Engineering and Science Hall of Fame in 1994. Robert Hayden wrote the following comment that spells out the significance of Gourdine's discoveries: 'The applications of electrogasdynamics developed by Gourdine have the potential of affecting the lives of generations of people to come. And, as we continue to struggle with the energy problem, the work of Meredith Gourdine cannot be overlooked.'

CHAPTER THREE: AFRICAN AMERICAN PIONEERS IN
MATHEMATICS AND PHYSICS

The Pioneers

The pioneering physicist, Edward Bouchet (1852-1918), was also the first African American to receive a PhD from an American university. Completing his physics dissertation through Yale's PhD program in 1876, Bouchet was among 20 Americans (of any race) to receive a PhD in physics. His thesis concerned measuring refractive indices. In more recent times, the American Physical Society offers the Edward A. Bouchet Award for outstanding contributions to physics. There is also the Edward Bouchet Abdus Salam Institute, founded in 1988 by the late Nobel Laureate, Professor Abdus Salam.

Dr Elbert Francis Cox (1896-1962) was the first African American PhD in mathematics. Qualifying at Cornel University in 1925, he was one of only 28 mathematics PhDs in the whole of the United States (of any race). He headed the mathematics department of Howard University for 32 years.

Figure 33. Dr Edward Bouchet (1852-1918), the first African American PhD in physics.

Dr J. Ernest Wilkins (1923-2011) was the second Black PhD in mathematics in the United States. He achieved his doctorate at the precocious age of 19 at the University of Chicago in 1942. In 1944 he returned to the University of Chicago where he served first as an associate mathematical physicist and then as a physicist in its Metallurgical Laboratory, as part of the Manhattan Project. Dr Wilkins researched the extraction of fissionable nuclear materials, but was not told of the research group's ultimate goal until after the atomic bomb was dropped on Hiroshima. Wilkins was the discoverer or co-discoverer of a number of phenomena in physics such as the Wilkins effect, also the Wigner-Wilkins and Wilkins spectra. Ultimately, he became a professor of applied mathematics and physics at Howard University.

Elmer Samuel Imes

Dr Elmer Samuel Imes (1883-1941) was a brilliant astro and industrial physicist. He made original and highly significant contributions to the development of the Quantum Theory. His research also addressed the problem of radiation. According to one writer: 'The consequences of his work are important today in two areas of technical concern; thermal

Figure 34. Dr Elmer Samuel Imes (1883-1941), brilliant astro and industrial physicist.

radiation from rocket engines using fluorine compounds as oxidizers, and radiation from chemical lasers based on hydrogenflourine reactions.'

Imes was born to college educated parents. He attended grammar school in Ohio and completed his high school education at the Agricultural and Mechanical High School in Norman, Alabama.

Imes graduated from Fisk University in 1903 with a degree in science. In 1918 he earned his PhD in physics at the University of Michigan where he studied under Dr Harrison McAllister Randall. Ultimately, he was the second African American to earn a PhD in physics. However, he was also among the first of the African American scientists to make important and lasting contributions to modern physics.

Imes' doctorate thesis led to the publication of *Measurements on the Near-Infrared Absorption of Some Diatomic Gases* in November 1919 in the *Astrophysical Journal*. Diatomic gases are gases made up of only two atoms. Imes followed this with a paper co-authored by Dr Harrison McAllister Randall *The Fine Structure of the Near Infra-Red Absorption Bands of HCl, HBr, and HF* for the American Physical Society and published in their *Physical Review* in 1920.

What is the importance of Dr Imes research? His research demonstrated for the first time that the Quantum Theory could be applied to radiation in all regions of the electromagnetic spectrum, to the rotational energy states of molecules, as well as the vibration and electronic levels. Thus, his work provided an early verification of the Quantum Theory.

Dr Imes produced other important ideas. His research was one of the earliest applications of high resolution infrared spectroscopy. Spectroscopy is the study of the relationship between matter and radiation. Imes research provided the first detailed spectra of molecules giving scientists a way to study the molecular structure of chemicals using infrared spectroscopy.

Despite his rare brilliance, Dr Imes was unable to secure employment in academia in the 1920s. Consequently, he became a physics consultant and researcher in physics for industry. During this period, he received four patents for instruments that measured electric and magnetic properties.

He was a member of various scientific societies including the American Institute of Electrical Engineers, the Sigma Xi, the American Physical Society and the American Society for Testing Materials.

Concerning the important role of African Americans in the more recent history of physics, Professor John Pappademos, an authority of African science history, wrote: 'Among Blacks living in the U.S. who have made important contributions to physics, the following are just a few: Meredith

Gourdine ... best known for his pioneering work in electrogasdynamics ... James Harris, co-discoverer of the trans-uranium elements 104 and 105; George Carruthers, designer of the far UV camera/spectrograph which was used in the earth's first moon-based observatory (Apollo 16) ... Earl Shaw ... a physicist at Bell Laboratories and who, in 1970, was the co-inventor of the spin-flip tunable Raman laser; Walter Massey, the scientific director of the leading energy research center in the U.S. (Argonne National Laboratory); and Shirley Jackson, who did research in the theory of elementary particles for two years at Fermilab and is now a scientist at Bell Laboratories.'

CHAPTER FOUR: AFRICAN AMERICAN PIONEERS IN BIOLOGY, BOTANY AND ZOOLOGY

George Washington Carver

Dr George Washington Carver (1860-1943) was a distinguished scientist of whom President Franklin D. Roosevelt wrote: 'All mankind is the beneficiary of his discoveries in the field of agricultural chemistry.' Henry Ford called him 'the greatest living scientist.' J. A. Rogers wrote: 'Carver revolutionized certain branches of agriculture in the southern United States, thereby benefitting millions of his fellow men in America and abroad. He was practically the founder of the $65,000,000 peanut industry of the Southern states.'

Born into captivity in Missouri, Carver became a free citizen when the American government passed the Thirteenth Amendment. As a young man, Carver excelled in fine art and science at Simpson College, Iowa. Taking courses in botany, geometry, chemistry, zoology, bacteriology and entomology, Carver achieved his Bachelor of Science in 1894.

After graduating, he worked at Iowa State College as an assistant botanist. Running a greenhouse, he soon grew 20,000 samples of fungi. He found ways of hybridising fruits and plants that made them resistant to

Figure 35. Dr George Washington Carver (1860-1943), 'the Wizard of Tuskegee' of whom Henry Ford called 'the greatest living scientist.'

fungus attack. Scientific journals began citing Carver as an authority. He earned the nickname 'The Plant Doctor.'

In 1896 he achieved his MA degree in agriculture and bacterial botany. That year, the great political leader and 'Sage of Tuskegee,' Booker T. Washington, recruited Carver to become the Director of Agriculture at Tuskegee. Here, he made additional scientific discoveries and earned the nickname 'The Wizard of Tuskegee.'

He made 325 products from and with peanuts. Among these were cream, buttermilk, instant coffee, face powder, printer's ink, butter, shampoo, vinegar, dyes, soap and wood stains. Southern farmers made more money from growing peanut crops rather than cotton and tobacco crops because of Carver's discoveries. However, J. A. Rogers detected a political agenda behind Dr Carver's discoveries. Growing cotton kept the Southern oligarchs rich and reduced their Black workers to semi-slavery. Carver's new discoveries undermined the cotton rich oligarchs.

Carver devised 118 products from or with sweet potato. Among these were flour, starch, tapioca, dyes, ink, and synthetic rubber. During World War I the US Army used his sweet potato to produce a cheaper loaf of bread.

He created 75 products from or with pecan. From waste materials such as corn stalks, he made hundreds of products. From cotton, he made insulating board, paper, rugs, cordage and paving blocks. From Alabama clay, he extracted beautiful dyes.

Yeboah gives additional examples of Dr Carver's genius: 'Some of his ideas took decades to materialise. He had made paper from the southern pine--and 25 years later his process led to a major new paper industry. He made synthetic marble from peanut shells and food wastes, and these discoveries presaged the fabrication of plastics from all sorts of vegetable matter. Substituting cellulose for steel, US car manufacturers would, in time, be building 350 pounds of agricultural products into every car ... He discovered during the First World War that he could reduce 100 pounds of sweet potatoes to a powder that fitted into a compact carton, kept indefinitely and could be instantly reconstituted by the addition of water. Today the dehydrated-food industry is worth billions of dollars ... From the Osange orange, he extracted a juice that tames the toughest cut of beef--one of the first meat tenderisers. He showed that the giant thistle--ranted at by farmers--contained medical properties, as did 250 other weeds he examined ... Another Carver experiment led to the now-standard use of soya bean oil as the base for car spray paints.'

In 1916 he was elected to be a Fellow of the Royal Society of Arts, Manufactures and Commerce of Great Britain. In 1939 he received the Theodore Roosevelt Medal 'for distinguished research in agricultural chemistry.' In 1940 Carver was chosen 'Man of the Year' by the International Federation of Architects, Engineers, Chemists and Technicians. A British MP said of him: "Parliament, when this war is over, should give thanks to Dr. Carver." Metro-Goldwyn-Mayer made a film about his life story. Finally, 5 January 1946 was hailed by Congress as George Washington Carver Day.

Charles Henry Turner

Dr Charles Henry Turner (1867-1923) was a prominent research biologist, zoologist, and comparative psychologist. His research gathered new information on the auditory, visual and learning abilities of insects.

For example, Dr Turner was the first to demonstrate that insects could hear. He also demonstrated that insects and surface-feeding caterpillars used trial-and-error learning. Moreover, he created complex apparati to show that ants use light in addition to scent trails to get back to their nest. Finally, he was the first to show that honeybees can see in colour.

Born in Missouri, he was the first African American to receive a graduate degree from the University of Cincinnati in 1892. Moreover, he was the first African American to earn a PhD from the University of Chicago in 1907. However, despite his doctorate, he taught at high schools since he was unable to get an academic appointment at the University of Chicago.

Figure 36. Dr Charles Henry Turner (1867-1923) was a prominent research biologist, zoologist, and comparative psychologist.

During his 33 year career, Dr Turner published more than 70 papers, many of them written while he confronted numerous challenges. Among these were restrictions on his access to laboratories and research libraries, and restrictions on his time due to a heavy teaching. Among his papers were *Hunting Habits of an American Sand Wasp, Habits of Mound-Building Ants, Experiments on the Color Vision of the Honeybee,* and *Psychological Notes on the Gallery Spider.*

Dr Turner designed mazes to study ants and cockroaches. He also designed coloured disks and boxes for testing the pattern and colour recognition of honeybees. He conducted naturalistic observations, and performed experiments on insect navigation, death feigning, and the basic problems in invertebrate learning. Turner may well have been the very first to investigate Pavlovian conditioning in an invertebrate. Moreover, he discovered that cockroaches trained to avoid a dark chamber in one apparatus retained that behaviour when transferred to a differently shaped apparatus.

Zoologists during his time still took their intellectual cues from the nineteenth century concepts of taxis and kinesis, in which social insects were thought to alter their behaviour in specific responses to specific stimuli. Through his observations, Dr Turner was able to establish that insects can learn and thus modify their behaviour as a result of experience.

Finally, Dr Turner was one of the first behavioural scientists to pay close attention to the use of controls and variables in experiments.

Ernest Everett Just

Dr Ernest Everett Just (1883-1941) was a pioneering biologist, academic and science writer. Just's primary legacy is his recognition of the fundamental role of the cell surface in the development of organisms. In his work within marine biology, cytology and parthenogenesis, he advocated the study of whole cells under normal conditions, rather than simply breaking them apart in a laboratory setting.

Born in South Carolina, he displayed exceptional brilliance as a pupil. He went on to graduate *magna cum laude* from Dartmouth College, Hanover, New Hampshire in 1907. He won special honours in zoology, but also distinguished himself in botany, history, and sociology. On graduating from Dartmouth, Just faced the same problems that dogged other Black college graduates of his time. No matter how brilliant they were, it was almost impossible for Blacks to become faculty members in most of the American

Figure 37. Dr Ernest Everett Just (1883-1941) was a pioneering biologist, academic and science writer.

universities. This issue also hurt the careers of Bouchet, Imes, Turner, Williams, etcetera.

Just took the best choice available to him and was appointed to a teaching position at the historically-Black Howard University in 1907. In 1910 he was put in charge of the newly formed biology department, and within a few years ultimately become head of Howard's Department of Zoology, a position he held until his death in 1941.

While teaching at Howard, Just was introduced to Dr Frank Lillie, chief of the Marine Biological Laboratory at Woods Hole, Massachusetts, who invited Just to spend his summers as his research assistant at the Laboratory. Just accepted this invitation in 1909 and spent nearly every summer for the next twenty years at that Laboratory. A few years later, taking a leave of absence from Howard, Just enrolled on an advanced academic program at the University of Chicago, receiving his PhD there in 1916 *magna cum laude*. His thesis concerned the mechanics of fertilization.

From 1915, his research articles appeared in biological journals, showing his expertise on fertilization, artificial parthenogenesis, cell division, and hydration and dehydration in living cells. He also wrote on the effect of ultraviolet rays in increasing chromosome number in animals and in altering the organisation of the egg with special reference to polarity. According to J. A. Rogers: 'In polarity fertilization, on which great emphasis is laid by those scientists in search of the origin of life, his work was appraised by his contemporaries as among the most important in the field, while some placed him first.'

His early writings beginning in 1912 concerned the point of entrance of the sperm into the eggs of the sand worm. Just found that this determined the way in which the egg would develop. This was the first of more than sixty papers written over the next twenty five years dealing with fertilisation and experimental parthenogenesis which is the development of an egg without fertilisation. His findings would ultimately correct some of the earlier work done by scholars such as Jacques Loeb.

Dr Just had new ideas on the operation of cells. Earlier biologists thought that the nucleus of the cell controlled and dominated all the activities of the cell. The cytoplasm which is the protoplasm or living substance in a cell outside of the nucleus was considered unimportant and merited little attention by biologists. Similarly, few biologists even mentioned the ectoplasm which was the outer surface of the cytoplasm.

Dr Just believed that the ectoplasm and cytoplasm deserved more scholarly attention. Researching the development of the egg cells of marine animals, he found that the ectoplasm was just as important as the nucleus. He also found that the cell as a living unit depended on the smooth cooperation between the nucleus and cytoplasm. Additionally, he discovered that because of its closer relationship to the outside environment, the ectoplasm was primarily responsible for whatever individuality and harmonious development the cell had.

Since these ideas contradicted the popular beliefs of earlier biologists, scholars had to reconsider many of their formerly held ideas. Later editions of textbooks were rewritten to incorporate Dr Just's findings.

According to Dr Haber, these discoveries were profound indeed: 'These findings affected scientists' thinking on such fundamental things as the real difference between living and nonliving things, the way to determine sex in advance, the key to evolution, and the difference between plant and animal life. They also had a great bearing on medicine through a new understanding of the functions of the liver, the kidneys, the pancreas, and other vital organs from the standpoint of a new relationship between the cell and its surroundings, through the ectoplasm. The bearing of these research findings on the fight against cancer was pointed out by some scientists.'

In the mid to late twenties, his work started to appear in German biological texts. He engaged in research at the Kaiser Wilhelm Institute for Biology in Germany and the Marine Biological Laboratory in Naples, Italy. In 1930 he was elected vice president of the American Society of Zoologists. That year he delivered a paper at the Eleventh International Congress of Zoologists at Padua, Italy. He spoke on 'The Role of Cortical Cytoplasm in Vital Phenomena.' However beginning in 1933, Dr Just ceased his work in Germany when the Nazis began to take the control of the country. He relocated his European-based studies to Paris.

Dr Just wrote two books, *Basic Methods for Experiments on Eggs of Marine Mammals* in 1922, and *The Biology of the Cell Surface* in 1939. In a 1943 edition of the *Journal of Nervous and Mental Diseases,* a reviewer wrote the following: 'His book, "The Biology of the Cell Structure," which synthesizes his life work, is a remarkable contribution of highest scientific order, of value and interest alike to scientists in general as well as to practicing physicians and psychiatrists ... He knew the animal egg as few scientists knew their material. It was a knowledge so intimate, so deep, so clear-visioned as to comprehend even to the minutest; in the intricacies of the workings of the cell he could envision a macrocosm with a microcosm.'

In 1996 the US Postal Service issued a commemorative stamp honouring Just.

CHAPTER FIVE: AFRICAN AMERICAN PIONEERS IN CHEMISTRY

Lloyd A. Hall

Dr Lloyd A. Hall (1894-1971) was a pioneering food chemist who coined the phrase: "More nutritious and appetizing food for longer life through food technology." He was an expert in meat proteins, colloids and emulsions, fats, oils, yeast food, bakery materials, protein hydrosalates, flavouring and seasoning of foods and beverages, food sterilisation, chemotherapeutic products, and many others.

The young Hall excelled in the sciences at High School. He majored in Chemistry at Northwestern University achieving a B.S. degree in 1916. According to the great researcher J. A. Rogers, he was also 'Assistant chief inspector of high explosives and research for United States government in World War I, and worked on secret war problems in World War II.'

He worked as Chief Chemist and Director of Research at the Griffith Laboratories where he enjoyed a brilliant career. He worked there from 1925 to 1959 where a particular concern was meat preservation.

Sodium chloride has been used since the ancient times to preserve meat. Moreover, sodium nitrate and nitrite has a beneficial effect on the colour

Figure 38. Dr Lloyd A. Hall (1894-1971), pioneering food chemist.

and appearance of preserved meat. Dr Hall found that when all three were combined in the preserving and curing of meat, the nitrite penetrated fastest, followed by the nitrate, followed by the chloride. This meant that the meat disintegrated before the chloride could preserve it.

A European chemist, Karl Max Seifert produced a solution to the problem of meat disintegration called flash drying and sold the patent to Griffith Laboratories where Dr Hall worked on it. Hall invented the ingenious idea of enclosing the nitrate and nitrite within the sodium chloride crystal. Dr Haber states: 'Hall's [improvement to] the flash dried crystals were far superior to any meat-curing salts ever produced and were widely used in the meat industry.'

However, when stored in drums or other containers, there was a problem of the salt mixture reacting with air and moisture to cake (i.e. to form a solid mass). Hall found that by adding a combination of glycerine, alkali metal tartrate and the softening of hard water stopped the caking from taking place. The salt solution produced flowed like water and did note cake.

Hall found that the available spices (cloves, cinnamon, ginger, paprika, allspice, sage, etcetera) used to preserve food contained spores of moulds, yeasts and bacteria that contaminated the food. Hall also found that dried onion and garlic also contaminated the food. To address this problem, Dr Hall used a gas called ethylene oxide--previously used to kill insects--to kill germs in food. Other researchers used the idea to create sterilized spices. Others used the idea to create sterilized drugs, medical supplies and cosmetics. According to Dr Haber: 'Hall's method is in general use throughout the country.'

Oxidisation of fats and oils causes spoilage or rancidity in food. However, antioxidants retard or prevent this from happening. Hall came up with a combination of sodium chloride, propylene glycol, propyl gallate and citric acid. According to Dr Haber: 'These antioxidants are in very wide use today in the food industry.' Moreover, the anti-ageing and other health benefits of antioxidants are widely recognised today.

By 1970, Dr Hall had about 105 US and foreign patents and wrote around 50 scientific papers. He was a Member of the Institute of Food Technologists from 1939. He was Editor of the *The Vitalizer,* the magazine of the Institute of Food Technologists from 1948. He was an Executive Board member of the Institute of Food Technologists between 1951 and 1955. He was also a Member of the Board of Directors of the American Institute of Chemists from 1955.

Percy Lavon Julian

Dr Percy Lavon Julian (1899-1975) was the pioneering soybean chemist. What Dr Carver had done for peanuts, he did the same for the soybean.

The son of a railway clerk, Julian studied at DePauw University achieving his Bachelor's degree in 1920. Julian achieved a Master's degree in chemistry from Harvard University in 1923 and a PhD in chemistry from Vienna in 1931. He worked at Howard, then DePauw Universities.

His early work concerned synthesizing physostigmine--an effective treatment for glaucoma. However, his work on the soybean was particularly distinguished. He used it to commercially coat paper in a cost-effective way. He used it to make aero-foam--used as an anti-fire agent by the US Navy.

He also used soybean to make synthetic male and female hormones in a cost effective way. This is a key development in the evolution of hormone replacement therapy. Moreover, the hormones are effective in the treatment of cancer. According to Dr Haber, 'Julian's synthesis of these hormones from the common soybean ranks among the outstanding achievements of organic chemistry.'

He also used soybean in synthesis with cortexolone to make synthetic cortisone. This proved effective in the treatment of rheumatoid arthritis in

Figure 39. Dr Percy Lavon Julian (1899-1975), pioneering soybean chemist.

a cost effective way. He thus broke the monopoly that European chemists had on the production of sterols. They extracted it from the bile of animals at an immense cost of hundreds of dollars per gram. Dr Julian's synthetic cortisone cost less than twenty cents a gram.

After forming his own company devoted to the production of sterols, Smith, Kline and French, a pharmaceutical company, bought him out in 1961. They paid him $2,338,000.

Dr Julian's research was widely celebrated. He was a Fellow of the Chemical Society of London, the New York Academy of Science and the American Institute of Chemists. In 1964 he received the Honor Scroll Award from the American Institute of Chemists. In 1968 he received the Chemical Pioneer Award from the American Institute of Chemists.

Lloyd Quarterman

Lloyd Quarterman (1918-1982) was a chemist best known for his contribution to the building of the atomic bomb during the World War II era. Called the Manhattan Project, he was one of twelve Black men of science involved in the project. He received a certificate of appreciation by the US Secretary of War for 'work essential to the production of the Atomic Bomb, thereby contributing to the successful conclusion of World War II.'

As a young boy Quarterman discovered a passion for science and spent many hours working with chemistry sets. During the 1930s, he went to college at St Augustines in Raleigh, North Carolina, earning a Bachelor's degree in 1943.

Even though he was just a graduate with only a Bachelor's degree, the United States War Department recruited him alongside eleven other African Americans to be involved with the atomic bomb project. He was officially an assistant to an associate research scientist and chemist. No one knows what his exact duties were since all were sworn to secrecy. The other African American scientists and mathematicians included Dr William Knox, Sidney Thomson, George Reed, Clarence Turner, Dr Moddie Taylor, Robert Omohundro, Sherman Carter, Jasper Jeffries, Benjamin Scott and Dr J. Ernest Wilkins. I, however, speculate that Dr Lloyd Hall also worked on this project since it is on record that he 'worked on secret war problems in World War II.'

Many different teams of scientists worked on the bomb project. Quarterman worked with scientists at Columbia University and at the University of Chicago. The Chicago team were the first to split the atom,

Figure 40. Lloyd Quarterman (1918-1982), chemist best known for his contribution to building the atomic bomb during World War II.

creating nuclear fission. Here, Quarterman occasionally worked alongside Albert Einstein to help create uranium isotopes, necessary for uranium gas, which made fission possible. Kept very secret, this project became known as the plutonium project. It was under this project that the first nuclear reactor was built. This is the most essential part of modern nuclear power plants.

In time the Chicago team became the Argonne National Laboratories. Funded by the University of Chicago, they researched peaceful uses for nuclear energy. Quarterman remained involved with this team for the next thirty years where they devised the nuclear reactor for the Nautilus, the famous nuclear powered submarine.

Quarterman was also known for his work as an inorganic chemist specialising in fluorides. His team created new chemical compounds and molecules from fluoride. Working with zeon, argon, and krypton, he made them react with fluorine, creating new compounds including zeon diflouride, zeon tetraflouride and zeon hexafluoride. Zeon, argon, and krypton were not known to react with anything before this. Hence they were called the 'noble gases,' i.e. too noble to react with anything else. Quarterman's team ultimately became the foremost fluoride chemists on earth.

Quarterman was also a spectroscopist, i.e. someone who studies how matter and radiation interact. According to Professor Van Sertima, editor of the superb *Blacks in Science: Ancient and Modern:* 'A spectroscopist is like a man peering into the depths of the universe with a dozen eyes or windows. With these marvellously revealing scopes, he can look through solutions or through various spectra or spheres into the living interaction or vibration of chemical or molecular or gaseous species. He can study the composition of elements in our universe that are either invisible or elusive or obscure to us. Sometimes he needs to make a new kind of eye or a new kind of window in order to observe and determine these things with greater precision.'

Consequently, in 1967 Quarterman's team created the diamond window. This made it possible for scientists to observe the X-ray, the ultraviolet region, or the Raman spectrum of various chemical compounds. His device made it possible to detect and observe the vibrations of molecules from each compound, enabling scientists to learn more about their molecular structures and manipulate them to create new chemical compounds (such as zeon diflouride, zeon tetraflouride and zeon hexafluoride, mentioned earlier).

However, hydrogen fluoride was so corrosive that it would even dissolve glass. Since Quarterman's diamond window was designed to largely withstand the corrosive effects of hydrogen fluoride, this enabled spectroscopists to observe and study, through an electro-magnetic beam, compounds dissolved in hydrogen fluoride. They were thus able to observing the vibrations of their molecules, learn about their structures and devise ways of manipulating them should it be necessary.

Quarterman was a member of the Scientific Research Society of America, the Society of Applied Spectroscopy, the Society of Sigma Xi, the American Chemical Society and the American Association for the Advancement of Science.

CHAPTER SIX: AFRICAN AMERICAN PIONEERS IN MEDICINE AND SURGERY

Daniel Hale Williams

Dr Daniel Hale Williams (1856-1931) was a pioneering surgeon who performed an early and completely successful open heart surgery as early as 1893!

Born in Pennsylvania, the young Williams was of very mixed ancestry (African, European and Native American on both sides of the family). Aged 10 the young Williams was an apprentice to a shoemaker. He then worked on lake steamers and eventually became a barber. Aged 22 he apprenticed in medicine under a physician called Dr Henry Palmer. At the age of 24 he studied at Chicago Medical School, graduating three years later. There, he became familiar with the 'new' ideas of Louis Pasteur (i.e. Germ Theory of Disease) and Joseph Lister (i.e. Effectiveness of Antiseptics).

Dr Williams began to work as a surgeon, performing operations at the patient's homes as was the general practise at that time. He scrupulously applied Lister's ideas of antiseptic surgery--scrubbing rooms, spraying carbolic acid and sterilizing all clothing and equipment.

He was much in demand and worked in a number of capacities. He was a surgeon for South Side Dispensary in Chicago. He taught anatomy at the Chicago Medical College. He was a surgeon to the City Railway Company. Moreover, he was a member of the Illinois State Board of Health

In May 1891 he opened the Provident Hospital and Training School Association. This was the first interracial hospital in the United States. It was also the first institution to train Black nurses in the United States.

On 9 July 1893 Dr Williams performed a surgical operation that made history. A certain James Cornish sustained a knife wound during a saloon bar fight. Cornish was rushed to Provident Hospital where Dr Williams leading a team of six colleagues attended to him. Dr Williams opened his chest cavity, examined the knife wound, concluded that the heart did not need suturing, and chose instead to suture the pericardium. This was a daring operation. The key question was: Would it work?

Unfortunately the patient died ...

... fifty years later!

Figure 41. The Provident Hospital and Training School Association.

The *Chicago Daily Inter-Ocean* reported the operation under the headline 'Sewed Up His Heart.' While not the first operation of its kind in the world, this does demonstrate how old open heart surgery is. Some writers suggest that Williams' operation may have been the second time that open-heart surgery had been performed in the United States.

In February 1894 Dr Williams became Chief Surgeon to the Freedmen's Hospital in Washington. In 1913 he became a Charter member of the American College of Surgeons.

William Augustus Hinton

Professor William Augustus Hinton (1883-1959) was the leading researcher in syphilis and gonococcus infection. His test for syphilis was at one time the standard one used by the Public Health Service across the United States.

Born in Chicago, Hinton's parents were former slaves. After high school, he studied at the University of Kansas, finishing his medical studies in just two years instead of the usual three. He continued undergraduate studies at Harvard, receiving a bachelor's degree in 1905.

In 1909 Hinton was offered a scholarship reserved for Black students, but refused it and instead, decided to compete for a scholarship open to all students. He won that scholarship two years in a row. Ultimately, he finished the Harvard medical program in just three years instead of the usual four. He received his MD qualification in 1912.

After graduating, he began work at the Wassermann Laboratory at Harvard becoming the director of the lab a few years later. This same lab was used by the Massachusetts State Department of Public Health. In 1916

Figure 42. Professor William Augustus Hinton (1883-1959).

he also became a pathologist and director of the Boston Dispensary's laboratory department. There he created a program to train women as lab technicians, thus opening the door to women.

For most of his research career, Dr Hinton worked on laboratory tests designed to improve the diagnosis of sexually transmitted diseases. In 1927 he developed a test, later known as the Hinton Test, for diagnosing syphilis. His test was easier, less expensive, and more accurate than previous methods reducing the number of false positive results. It thus became the standard procedure for diagnosing syphilis.

How did it work? A newspaper article explains: 'Dr. Hinton's test consists in putting a small quantity of the patient's blood serum in a test tube and adding glycerine, ether, salt, and extract of beef heart muscle. The mixture is allowed to stand for eighteen hours and if it clears and deposits a ring of white particles at the top, then the patient has syphilis. The U.S. Public Health Service and the American Society of Pathologists examined four kinds of blood tests in 1934 and rated Hinton's the most accurate.'

Later, Dr Hinton helped to develop another diagnostic test known as the Davies-Hinton Test.

As a professor, Hinton taught preventative medicine and hygiene at Harvard from 1923 onwards, staying in that post for twenty seven years. His book on syphilis, *Syphilis and its Treatment,* became widely acclaimed. The first medical textbook by an African American, Hinton noted the role of socioeconomics in health. He designated syphilis as 'a disease of the underprivileged.' He also worked as a special consultant to the US Public Health Service and taught at Tufts University and Simmons College.

Charles Richard Drew

Professor Charles Richard Drew (1904-1950) was a pioneering surgeon who headed the US and UK Blood Banks during World War II. His techniques saved untold numbers of lives during that conflict. He was the world's leading authority on blood plasma, serum, blood preservation and blood substitutes.

Born in Washington, DC, the young Drew was distinguished as an athlete in his school days. He displayed talent in football, basketball, baseball and track. Initially, he taught athletics and biology at Morgan State College from 1926 to 1928. Around 1929 he entered McGill University Medical School in Canada. There he studied Dr Karl Landsteiner's theories of the division of blood types into A, B, AB and O.

Figure 43. Professor Charles Richard Drew (1904-1950), pioneering surgeon who headed the US and UK Blood Banks during World War II.

Between 1938 and 1940, he attended Columbia University where he wrote a paper called 'The Early Recognition and Treatment of Shock.'

However, his main area of research concerned blood preservation. He studied the early attempts of blood banks in the USSR and Republican Spain. He found that using blood plasma (i.e. the liquid portion of the blood without the cells) was better for transfusions than using whole blood. He achieved the ScD degree in medicine for the thesis 'Banked Blood: A Study of Blood Preservation.'

At the request of his old British teacher at McGill University, Drew headed the 'Blood for Britain' initiative in August 1940. Following this, the Board of the Blood Transfusion Association in New York offered Drew the soon to be created position of Full-time Medical Supervisor of the project. In offering him the project the request read as follows: 'I am requested to offer this position and all it involves to you as being the best qualified of anyone we know to act in this important development.' The American Red Cross appointed Drew as Director of the US national blood collection for the US armed forces. However, despite this, the Americans continued to segregate blood by race!

He became Professor of Surgery at Howard University. In 1946 he was elected Fellow of the International College of Surgeons. Three years later, he was appointed Surgical Consultant for the US Army's Theatre of Operation.

APPENDICES

Commentary on *Theo's Story*

Below, I have included a story that has been doing the rounds for a few years now. Called *Theo's Story,* it is also known as *A World without Black People.* The tale presents some of the contributions of African Americans to science and invention in an easily digestible form. This is admirable since the story gives examples not mentioned anywhere else in this book. However, there are problems with this story that need to be addressed.

Firstly, *Theo's Story* fails to distinguish between inventing *A* device and inventing *THE* device. As I have said in Chapter 2, many devices have been invented several times by many different inventors and in many different countries. Moreover, the prototypes of many non-electronic devices were actually pioneered in the ancient civilisations. For instance, *Theo's Story* references Walter Sammons in the invention of the comb. Certainly, Walter Sammons invented *A* comb, but did he invent *THE* comb? Combs have been around in every civilisation going back to the Ancient Egyptians.

Secondly, *Theo's Story* implies that without the African American inventors, no one else would have invented these devices and thus society would have been in the dark. While there are some examples where this is undoubtedly true, there are many more examples where others in other countries, times and places made similar innovations.

Thirdly, there is a strong element of spin in *Theo's Story* where the lack of an invention is linked to the lack of the product itself. For instance *Theo's Story* implies that had Matzeliger not invented the lasting machine, then shoes would not exist today. The reality is that shoes would have existed, but they would have been much more expensive.

Fourthly, critics of *Theo's Story* who accuse African Americans of exaggerations, conclude that Black people were a negligible factor in the history of science and invention. This is not true. What these critics fail to understand is that the world is bigger than Europe. It is also bigger than European America. Amongst the ancient civilisations and early peoples that pioneered science and invention were Africans from Africa. Readers who want to pursue this should read some of the other books in this series.

With these provisos in mind, enjoy *Theo's Story.*

Theo's Story

This is a story of a little boy name Theo, who woke up one morning and asked his mother, "Mom, what if there were no Black people in the world?" Well, his mother thought about that for a moment, and then said, "Son, follow me around today and let's just see what it would be like if there were no Black people in the world." Mom said, "Now go get dressed, and we will get started."

Theo ran to his room to put on his clothes and shoes. His mother took one look at him and said, "Theo, where are your shoes? And those clothes are all wrinkled, son. I must iron them." However, when she reached for the ironing board, it was no longer there.

You see Sarah Boone, a black woman, invented the ironing board, and Jan E. Matzeliger, a black man, invented the shoe lasting machine.

"Oh well," she said, "please go and do something to your hair." Theo ran in his room to comb his hair, but the comb was not there. You see, Walter Sammons, a black man, invented the comb.

Theo decided to just brush his hair, but the brush was gone. You see Lydia O. Newman, a black female, invented the brush.

Well, this was a sight: no shoes, wrinkled clothes, hair a mess. Even Mom's hair, without the hair care inventions of Madam C. J. Walker, well, you get the picture.

Mom told Theo, "Let's do our chores around the house and then take a trip to the grocery store." Theo's job was to sweep the floor. He swept and swept and swept. When he reached for the dustpan, it was not there. You see, Lloyd P. Ray, a black man, invented the dustpan.

So he swept his pile of dirt over in the corner and left it there. He then decided to mop the floor, but the mop was gone. You see, Thomas W. Stewart, a black man, invented the mop. Theo yelled to his Mom, "Mom, I'm not having any luck."

"Well, son," she said, "Let me finish washing these clothes, and we will prepare a list for the grocery store." When the wash finished, she went to place the clothes in the dryer, but it was not there. You see, George T. Samon, a black man, invented the clothes dryer.

Mom asked Theo to go get a pencil and some paper to prepare their list for the market. So, Theo ran for the paper and pencil but noticed the pencil lead was broken. Well, he was out of luck because John Love, a black man, invented the pencil sharpener.

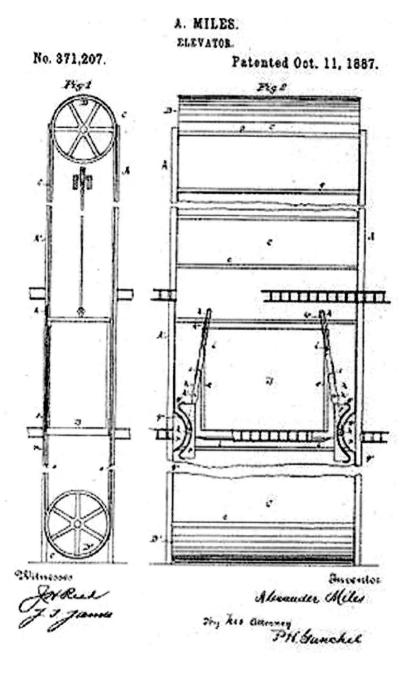

Figure 44. Patent of an Elevator invented by Alexander Miles number 371,207, received 11 October 1887.

Mom reached for a pen, but it was not there because William Purvis, a black man, invented the fountain pen.

As a matter of fact, Lee Burridge invented the typewriting machine and W. A. Lovette the advanced printing press. Theo and his mother decided just to head out to the market.

Well, when Theo opened the door, he noticed the grass was as high as he was tall. You see, John Burr, a black man, invented the lawn mower. They made their way over to the car and found that it just wouldn't go. You see, Richard Spikes, a black man, invented the automatic gearshift, and Joseph Gammel invented the supercharge system for internal combustion engines. They also noticed that the few cars that were moving were running into each other and having wrecks because there were no traffic signals. You see, Garrett A. Morgan, a black man invented the traffic light.

Well, it was getting late, so they walked to the market, got their groceries, and returned home. Just when they were about to put away the milk, eggs, and butter, they noticed the refrigerator was gone. You see John Standard, a black man, invented the refrigerator. So, they just left the food on the counter.

By this time, Theo noticed he was getting mighty cold. Mom went to turn up the heat, and what do you know? Alice Parker, a black female, invented the heating furnace. Even in the summertime, they would have been out of luck because Frederick Jones, a black man, invented the air conditioner.

It was almost time for Theo's father to arrive home. He usually takes the bus, but there was no bus, because its precursor was the electric trolley, invented by another black man, Elbert R. Robinson.

He usually takes the elevator from his office on the 20th floor, but there was no elevator because Alexander Miles, a black man, invented the elevator.

He also usually dropped off the office mail at a near by mailbox, but it was no longer there because Philip Downing, a black man, invented the letter drop mailbox, and William Barry invented the postmarking and cancelling machine.

Theo and his mother sat at the kitchen table with their heads in their hands. When father arrived, he asked, "Why are you sitting in the dark?" Why? Because Lewis Howard Latimer, a black man, invented the filament within the light bulb.

Theo quickly learned more about what it would be like if there were no black people in the world, especially if he were ever sick and needed blood. Dr. Charles Drew, a black scientist, found a way to preserve and store blood, which led to his starting the world's first blood bank.

Well, what if a family member had to have heart surgery? This would not have been possible without Dr. Daniel Hale Williams, a black doctor, who performed the first open-heart surgery.

So, if you ever wonder, like Theo, where would we be without black people? Well, it's pretty plain to see. We would still be in the DARK!

Introduction to *The Colored Inventor*

In 1913 Henry E. Baker wrote the classic pamphlet on African American inventors, *The Colored Inventor: A Record of Fifty Years.* A superb work, the pamphlet mentions African American inventors, some of whom I have written about in Chapter 2 of this book. What follows below, are the inventors that Baker documents that I have NOT mentioned in Chapter 2 or anywhere elsewhere in this text. I have thus edited the pamphlet to remove information that is duplicated elsewhere. I have left in his superb introduction and his inspiring conclusion since they give great context to the lives and achievements of the Black pioneers of invention.

Excerpts from *The Colored Inventor*

THE year 1913 marks the close of the first fifty years since Abraham Lincoln issued that famous edict known as the emancipation proclamation, by which physical freedom was vouchsafed to the slaves and the descendants of slaves in this country. And it would seem entirely fit and proper that those who were either directly or indirectly benefited by that proclamation should pause long enough at this period in their national life to review the past, recount the progress made, and see, if possible, what of the future is disclosed in the past.

That the colored people in the United States have made substantial progress in the general spread of intelligence among them, and in elevating the tone of their moral life; in the acquisition of property; in the development and support of business enterprises, and in the professional activities, is a matter of quite common assent by those who have been at all observant on the subject. This fact is amply shown to be true by the many universities, colleges and schools organized, supported and manned by the race, by their attractive homes and cultured home life, found now in all parts of our country; by the increasing numbers of those of the race who are successfully engaging in professional life, and by the gradual advance the race is making toward business efficiency in many varied lines of business activity.

It is not so apparent, however, to the general public that along the line of inventions also the colored race has made surprising and substantial progress; and that it has followed, even if "afar off," the footsteps of the more favored race. And it is highly important, therefore, that we should make note of what the race has achieved along this line to the end that proper credit may be accorded it as having made some contribution to our national progress.

Standing foremost in the list of things that have actually done most to promote our national progress in all material ways is the item of inventions. Without inventions we should have had no agricultural implements with which to till the fertile fields of our vast continent; no mining machinery for recovering the rich treasure that for centuries lay hidden beneath our surface; no steamcar or steamboat for transporting the products of field and mine; no machinery for converting those products into other forms of commercial needs; no telegraph or telephone for the speedy transmission of messages, no means for discovering and controlling the various utilitarian applications of electricity; no one of those delicate instruments which enable the skilful surgeon of to-day to transform and renew the human body, and often to make life itself stand erect, as it were, in the very presence of death. Without inventions we could have none of those numerous instruments which to-day in the hands of the scientist enable him accurately to forecast the weather, to anticipate and provide against storms on land and at sea, to detect seismic disturbances and warn against the dangers incident to their repetition; and no wireless telegraphy with its manifold blessings to humanity.

All these great achievements have come to us from the hand of the inventor. He it is who has enabled us to inhabit the air above us, to tunnel the earth beneath, explore the mysteries of the sea, and in a thousand ways, unknown to our forefathers, multiply human comforts and minimize human misery. Indeed, it is difficult to recall a single feature of our national progress along material lines that has not been vitalized by the touch of the inventor's genius.

Into this vast yet specific field of scientific industry the colored man has, contrary to the belief of many, made his entry, and has brought to his work in it that same degree of patient inquisitiveness, plodding industry and painstaking experiment that has so richly rewarded others in the same line of endeavor, namely, the endeavor both to create new things and to effect such new combinations of old things as will adapt them to new uses. We know that the colored man has accomplished something-indeed, a very great deal-in the field of invention, but it would be of the first importance to us now to know exactly what he has done, and the commercial value of his productions. Unfortunately for us, however, this can never be known in all its completeness.

A very recent experiment in the matter of collecting information on this subject has disclosed some remarkably striking facts, not the least interesting of which is the very widespread belief among those who ought to know better that the colored man has done absolutely nothing of value in the line of invention. This is but a reflex of the opinions variously expressed by others at different times on the subject of the capacity of the colored man for mental work of a high order. Thomas Jefferson's remark that no colored man could probably be found who was capable of taking in and comprehending Euclid, and that none had made any contribution to the civilization of the world through his art, would perhaps appear somewhat excusable when viewed in the light of the prevailing conditions in his day, and on which, of course, his judgment was based; but even at that time Jefferson knew something of the superior quality of Benjamin Banneker's mental equipment, for it is on record that they exchanged letters on that subject.

Coming down to a later day, when our race as a whole had shared, to some extent at least, in the progress of learning, so well informed an exponent of popular thought as Henry Ward Beecher is said to have declared that the whole African race in its native land could be obliterated from the face of the earth without loss to civilization, and yet Beecher knew, or should have known, of the scholarly Dr. Blyden, of Liberia, who was at one time president of the college of Liberia at Monrovia, and minister from his country to the Court of St. James, and whose contributions to the leading magazines of Europe and America were eagerly accepted and widely read on both continents.

Less than ten years ago, in a hotly contested campaign in the State of Maryland, a popular candidate for Congress remarked, in one of his speeches, that the colored race should be denied the right to vote because "none of them had ever evinced sufficient capacity to justify such a privilege," and that "no one of the race had ever yet reached the dignity of an inventor." Yet, at that very moment, there was in the Library of Congress in Washington a book of nearly 500 pages containing a list of nearly 400 patents representing the inventions of colored people.

Only a few years later a leading newspaper in the city of Richmond, Va., made the bold statement that of the many thousands of patents annually granted by our government to the inventors of our country, "not a single patent had ever been granted to a colored man." Of course this statement was untrue, but what of that? It told its tale, and made its impression-far and wide; and it is incumbent upon our race now to outrun that story, to correct that impression, and to let the world know the truth.

In a recent correspondence that has reached nearly two-thirds of the more than 12,000 registered patent attorneys in this country, who are licensed to prosecute applications for patents before the Patent Office at Washington, it is astonishing to have nearly 2,500 of them reply that they never heard of a colored inventor, and not a few of them add that they never expect to hear of one. One practising attorney, writing from a small town in Tennessee, said that he not only has never heard of a colored man inventing anything, but that he and the other lawyers to whom he passed the inquiry in that locality were "inclined to regard the whole subject as a joke." And this, remember, comes from practising lawyers, presumably men of affairs, and of judgment, and who keep somewhat ahead of the average citizen in their close observation of the trend of things.

Now there ought not to be anything strange or unbelievable in the fact that in any given group of more than 10,000,000 human beings, of whatever race, living in our age, in our country, and developing under our laws, one can find multiplied examples of every mental bent, of every stage of mental development, and of every evidence of mental perception that could be found in any other similar group of human beings of any other race; and yet, so set has become the traditional attitude of one class in our country toward the other class that the one class continually holds up before its eyes an imaginary boundary line in all things mental, beyond which it seems unwilling to admit that it is possible for the other class to go.

Under this condition of the general class thought in our country it has become the fixed conviction that no colored man has any well-defined power of initiative, that the colored man has no originality of thought, that in his mental operations he is everlastingly content to pursue the beaten paths of imitation, that therefore he has made no contribution to the inventive genius of our country, and so has gained no place for himself in the ranks of those who have made this nation the foremost nation of the world in the number and character of its inventions.

That this conclusion with reference to the colored man's inventive faculty is wholly untrue I will endeavor now to show.

In the world of invention the colored man has pursued the same line of activity that other men have followed; he has been spurred by the same necessity that has confronted other men, namely, the need for some device by which to minimize the exactions of his daily toil, to save his time, conserve his strength and multiply the results of his labor. Like other men, the colored man sought first to invent the thing that was related to his earlier occupations, and as his industrial pursuits became more varied his inventive genius widened correspondingly. Thus we find that the first recorded instances of patents having been granted to a colored man--and the only ones specifically so designated--are the two patents on corn harvesters which were granted in 1834 and 1836 to one Henry Blair, of Maryland, presumably a "free person of color," as the law was so construed at that time as to bar the issuance of a patent to a slave.

With the exception of these two instances the public records of the Patent Office give absolutely no hint as to whether any one of the more than 1,000,000 patents granted by this government to meritorious inventors from all parts of the world has been granted to a colored inventor. The records make clear enough distinctions as to nationality, but absolutely none as to race. This policy of having the public records distinguish between inventors of different nationalities only is a distinct disadvantage to the colored race in this country.

If the inventors of England or France or Germany or Italy, or any other country, desire to ascertain the number and character of the inventions patented to the citizens of their respective countries, it would require but a few hours of work to get exact statistics on the subject, but not so with the colored inventor. Here, as elsewhere, he has a hard road to travel.

In fact, it seems absolutely impossible to get even an approximately correct answer to that question for our race. Whatever of statistics one is able to get on this subject must be obtained almost wholly in a haphazard sort of way from persons not employed in the Patent Office, and who must, in the great majority of cases, rely on their memory to some extent for the facts they give. Under such circumstances as these it is easy to see the large amount of labor involved in getting up such statistics as may be relied upon as being true.

There have been two systematic efforts made by the Patent Office itself to get this information, one of them being in operation at the present time. The effort is made through a circular letter addressed to the thousands of patent attorneys throughout the country, who come in contact often with inventors as their clients, to popular and influential newspapers, to conspicuous citizens of both races, and to the owners of large manufacturing industries where skilled mechanics of both races are employed, all of whom are asked to report what they happen to know on the subject under inquiry.

The answers to this inquiry cover a wide range of guesswork, many mere rumors and a large number of definite facts. These are all put through the test of comparison with the official records of the Patent Office, and this sifting process has evolved such facts as form the basis of the showing presented here.

There is just one other source of information which, though its yield of facts is small, yet makes up in reliability what it lacks in numerousness; and that is where the inventor himself comes to the Patent Office to look after his invention. This does not often happen, but it rarely leaves anything to the imagination when it does happen.

Sometimes it has been difficult to get this information by correspondence even from colored inventors themselves. Many of them refuse to acknowledge that their inventions are in any way identified with the colored race, on the ground, presumably, that the publication of that fact might adversely affect the commercial value of their invention; and in view of the prevailing sentiment in many sections of our country, it cannot be denied that much reason lies at the bottom of such conclusion.

Notwithstanding the difficulties above mentioned as standing in the way of getting at the whole truth, something over 1,200 instances have been gathered as representing patents granted to colored inventors, but so far only about 800 of these have been verified as definitely belonging to that class.

These 800 patents tell a wonderful story of the progress of the race in the mastery of the science of mechanics. They cover inventions of more or less importance in all the branches of mechanics, in chemical compounds, in surgical instruments, in electrical utilities, and in the fine arts as well.

From the numerous statements made by various attorneys to the effect that they have had several colored clients whose names they could not recall, and whose inventions they could not identify on their books, it is practically certain that the nearly 800 verified patents do not represent more than one-half of those that have been actually granted to colored inventors, and that the credit for these must perhaps forever lie hidden in the unbreakable silence of official records.

But before directing attention specifically to some of the very interesting details disclosed by this latest investigation into the subject, let us consider for a brief moment a few of the inventions which colored men have made, but for which no patents appear to be of record.

I should place foremost among these that wonderful clock constructed by our first astronomer, Benjamin Banneker, of Maryland ...

Another instance is that of Mr. James Forten, of Philadelphia, who is credited with the invention of an apparatus for managing sails. He lived from 1766 to 1842, and his biographer says he amassed a competence from his invention and lived in leisurely comfort as a consequence.

Still another instance is that of Robert Benjamin Lewis, who was born in Gardiner, Me., in 1802. He invented a machine for picking oakum, which machine is said to be in use to-day in all the essential particulars of its original form by the shipbuilding interests of Maine, especially at Bath.

It is of common knowledge that in the South, prior to the War of the Rebellion, the burden of her industries, mechanical as well as agricultural, fell upon the colored population. They formed the great majority of her mechanics and skilled artisans as well as of her ordinary laborers, and from this class of workmen came a great variety of the ordinary mechanical appliances, the invention of which grew directly out of the problems presented by their daily employment.

There has been a somewhat persistent rumor that a slave either invented the cotton gin or gave to Eli Whitney, who obtained a patent for it, valuable suggestions to aid in the completion of that invention. I have not been able to find any substantial proof to sustain that rumor. Mr. Daniel Murray, of the Library of Congress, contributed a very informing article on that subject to the *Voice of the Negro,* in 1905, but Mr. Murray did not reach conclusions favorable to the contention on behalf of the colored man.

It is said that the zigzag fence, so commonly used by farmers and others, was originally introduced into this country by African slaves.

We come now to consider the list of more modern inventions, those inventions from which the element of uncertainty is wholly eliminated, and which are represented in the patent records of our government.

In this verified list of nearly 800 patents granted by our government to the inventors of our race we find that they have applied their inventive talent to the whole range of inventive subjects; that in agricultural implements, in wood and metal-working machines, in land conveyances on road and track, in seagoing vessels, in chemical compounds, in electricity through all its wide range of uses, in aeronautics, in new designs of house furniture and bric-à-brac, in mechanical toys and amusement devices, the colored inventor has achieved such success as should present to the race a distinctly hope-inspiring spectacle.

Of course it is not possible, in this particular presentation of the subject, to dwell much at length upon the merits of any considerable number of individual cases. This feature will be brought out more fully in the larger publication on this subject which the writer now has in course of preparation. But there are several conspicuous examples of success in this line of endeavor that should be fully emphasized in any treatment of this subject ...

Foremost among these men in the number and variety of his inventions, as well as in the commercial value involved, stands the name of Granville T. Woods ...

In the prolific yield of his inventive genius, Elijah McCoy, of Detroit, stands next to Granville T. Woods ...

Another inventor whose patents occupy a conspicuous place in the records of the Patent Office, and whose achievements in that line stand recorded as a credit to the colored man, is Mr. William B. Purvis, of Philadelphia. His inventions also cover a variety of subjects, but are directed mainly along a single line of experiment and improvement. He began, in 1882, the invention of machines for making paper bags, and his improvements in this line of machinery are covered by a dozen patents; and a half dozen other patents granted Mr. Purvis include three patents on electric railways, one on a fountain pen, another on a magnetic car-balancing device, and still another for a cutter for roll holders.

Another very interesting instance of an inventor whose genius for creating new things is constantly active, producing results that express themselves in terms of dollars for himself and others, is that of Mr. Joseph Hunter Dickinson, of New Jersey. Mr. Dickinson's specialty is in the line of musical instruments, particularly the piano. He began more than fifteen years ago to invent devices for automatically playing the piano, and is at present in the employ of a large piano factory, where his various inventions in piano-player mechanism are eagerly adopted in the construction of some of the finest player pianos on the market. He has more than a dozen patents to his credit already, and is still devoting his energies to that line of invention.

The company with which he is identified is one of the very largest corporations of its kind in the world, and it is no little distinction to have one of our race occupy so significant a relation to it, and to hold it by the sheer force of a trained and active intellect.

Mr. Frank J. Ferrell, of New York, has obtained about a dozen patents for his inventions, the larger portion of them being for improvements in valves for steam engines.

Mr. Benjamin F. Jackson, of Massachusetts, is the inventor of a dozen different improvements in heating and lighting devices, including a controller for a trolley wheel.

Mr. Charles V. Richey, of Washington, has obtained about a dozen patents on his inventions, the last of which was a most ingenious device for registering the calls on a telephone and detecting the unauthorized use of that instrument. This particular patent was only recently taken out by Mr. Richey, and he has organized a company for placing the invention on the market, with fine prospects of success.

Hon. George W. Murray, of South Carolina, former member of Congress from that State, has received eight patents for his inventions in agricultural implements, including mostly such different attachments as readily adapt a single implement to a variety of uses.

Henry Creamer, of New York, has made seven different inventions in steam traps, covered by as many patents, and Andrew J. Beard, of Alabama, has about the same number to his credit for inventions in car-coupling devices.

Mr. William Douglass, of Kansas, was granted about a half dozen patents for various inventions in harvesting machines. One of his patents, that one numbered 789,010, and dated May 2, 1905, for a self-binding harvester, is conspicuous in the records of the Patent Office for the complicated and intricate character of the machine, for the extensive drawings required to illustrate it and the lengthy specifications required to explain it-there being thirty-seven large sheets of mechanical drawings and thirty-two printed pages of descriptive matter, including the 166 claims drawn to cover the novel points presented. This particular patent is, in these respects, quite unique in the class here considered.

Mr. James Doyle, of Pittsburgh, has obtained several patents for his inventions, one of them being for an automatic serving system. This latter device is a scheme for dispensing with the use of waiters in dining rooms, restaurants and at railroad lunch counters. It was recently exhibited with the Pennsylvania Exposition Society's exhibits at Pittsburgh, where it attracted widespread attention from the press and the public. The model used on that occasion is said to have cost nearly $2,000.

In the civil service at Washington there are several colored men who have made inventions of more or less importance which were suggested by the mechanical problems arising in their daily occupations.

Mr. Shelby J. Davidson, of Kentucky, a clerk in the office of the Auditor for the Post Office Department, operated a machine for tabulating and totalizing the quarterly accounts which were regularly submitted by the postmasters of the country. Mr. Davidson's attention was first directed to the loss in time through the necessity for periodically stopping to manually dispose of the paper coming from the machine. He invented a rewind device which served as an attachment for automatically taking up the paper as it issued from the machine, and adapted it for use again on the reverse side, thus effecting a very considerable economy of time and material. His main invention, however, was a novel attachment for adding machines which was designed to automatically include the government fee, as well as the amount sent, when totalizing the money orders in the reports submitted by postmasters. This was a distinct improvement in the efficiency and value of the machine he was operating and the government granted him patents on both inventions. His talents were recognized not only by the office in which he was employed by promotion in rank and pay, but also in a very significant way by the large factory which turned out the adding machines the government was using. Mr. Davidson has since resigned his position and is now engaged in the practice of the law in Washington, D. C.

Mr. Robert Pelham, of Detroit, is similarly employed in the Census Bureau, where his duties include the compilation of groups of statistics on sheets from data sent into the office from the thousands of manufacturers of the country. Unlike most of the other men in the departmental service, Mr. Pelham seemed anxious to get through with his job quickly, for he devised a machine used as an adjunct in tabulating the statistics from the manufacturers' schedules in a way that displaced a dozen men in a given quantity of work, doing the work economically, speedily and with faultless precision, when operated under Mr. Pelham's skilful direction. Mr. Pelham has also been granted a patent for his invention, and the proved efficiency of his devices induced the United States government to lease them from him, paying him a royalty for their use, in addition to his salary for operating them.

Mr. Pelham's mechanical genius is evidently "running in the family," for his oldest son, now a high-school youth, has distinguished himself by his experiments in wireless telegraphy, and is one of the very few colored boys in Washington holding a regular license for operating the wireless.

Mr. W. A. Lavalette, of the Government Printing Office, the largest printing establishment in the world, began his career as a printer there years before the development of that art called into use the wonderful machines employed in it to-day; and one of his first efforts was to devise a printing machine superior to the pioneer type used at that time. This was in 1879, and he succeeded that year in inventing and patenting a printing machine that was a notable novelty in its day, though it has, of course, long ago been superseded by others.

I have reserved for the last the name and work of Jan Matzeliger, of Massachusetts ...

Matzeliger was as truly a pioneer, blazing the way for a great industrial triumph, as was Whitney, or Howe, or Watt, or Fulton, or any other one of the scores of pioneers in the field of mechanical genius. The cotton gin of to-day is, of course, not the cotton gin first given to the world by Whitney, but the essential principles of its construction are found clearly outlined in Whitney's machine. The complex and intricate sewing machine of to-day, with its various attachments to meet the needs of the modern seamstress, is not the crude machine that came from the brain of Elias Howe; the giant locomotives that now speedily cover the transcontinental distance between New York and San Francisco bear but slight resemblance to the engine that Stephenson first gave us. In fact, the first productions of all these pioneers, while they disclosed the principles and laid the foundations upon which to build, resemble the later developments only "as mists resemble rain;" but these pioneers make up the army of capable men whose toil and trial, whose brawn and brain, whose infinite patience and indomitable courage have placed this nation of ours in the very front rank of the world's inventors; and, standing there among them, with his name indelible, is our dark-skinned brother, the patient, resourceful Matzeliger.

In the credit here accorded our race for its achievements in the field of invention our women as well as our men are entitled to share. With an industrial field necessarily more circumscribed than that occupied by our men, and therefore with fewer opportunities and fewer reasons, as well, for exercising the inventive faculty, they have, nevertheless, made a remarkably creditable showing. The record shows that more than twenty colored women have been granted patents for their inventions, and that these inventions cover also a wide range of subjects-artistic, utilitarian, fanciful.

The foregoing facts are here presented as a part only of the record made by the race in the field of invention for the first half century of our national life. We can never know the whole story. But we know enough to feel sure that if others knew the story even as we ourselves know it, it would present us in a somewhat different light to the judgment of our fellow men, and, perhaps, make for us a position of new importance in the industrial activities of our country. This great consummation, devoutly to be wished, may form the story of the next fifty years of our progress along these specific lines, so that some one in the distant future, looking down the rugged pathway of the years, may see this race of ours coming up, step by step, into the fullest possession of our industrial, economic and intellectual emancipation.

THE AUTHOR: ROBIN WALKER

Biography

Robin Walker 'The Black History Man' was born in London but has also lived in Jamaica. He attended the London School of Economics and Political Science where he read Economics.

In 1991 and 1992, he studied African World Studies with the brilliant Dr Femi Biko and later with Mr Kenny Bakie. Between 1993 and 1994, he trained as a secondary school teacher at Edge Hill College (linked to the University of Lancaster).

Since 1992 and up to the present period, Robin Walker has lectured in adult education, taught university short courses, and chaired conferences in African World Studies, Egyptology and Black History. The venues have been in Toxteth (Liverpool), Manchester, Leeds, Bradford, Huddersfield, Birmingham, Cambridge, Buckinghamshire and London.

Since 1994 he has taught Economics, Business & Finance, Mathematics, Information Communications Technology, PSHE/Citizenship and also History at various schools in London and Essex.

In 1999 he wrote *Classical Splendour: Roots of Black History* published in the UK by Bogle L'Ouverture Publications. In the same year, he co-authored (with Siaf Millar) *The West African Empire of Songhai,* a textbook used by many schools across the country.

In 2000 he co-authored (again with Siaf Millar) *Sword, Seal and Koran,* another book on the Songhai Empire of West Africa.

In 2006 he wrote the seminal *When We Ruled.* This was the most advanced synthesis on Ancient and Mediaeval African history ever written by a single author. It was a massive expansion on his earlier book *Classical Splendour: Roots of Black History* and established his reputation as the leading Black History educational service provider.

In 2008 he wrote *Before The Slave Trade,* a highly pictorial companion volume to *When We Ruled.*

In 2013, he co-authored (with Siaf Millar and Saran Keita) *Everyday Life In An Early West African Empire.* It was a massive expansion on the earlier book *Sword, Seal & Koran.* Also this same year, he turned one of his e-books into the very book that you are holding right now.

Speaking Engagements

Looking for a speaker for your next event?

The author Robin Walker 'The Black History Man' is dynamic and engaging, both as a speaker and a workshop leader. He brings Black or African history alive, making it relevant for the present generation. You will love his perfect blend of accessibility, engagement, and academic rigour where learning becomes fun.

Walker is available to give speaking engagements to a variety of audiences.

Motivational crowds, general audiences, schools and parents will enjoy Walker's highly engaging presentation *Inspirational Black Pioneers of Science and Invention.*

To book Robin Walker for your next event, send an email to historicalwalker@yahoo.com

Short Course on Black History in Science

Would you like to deepen your learning in Black history by studying with Robin Walker?

As part of his mission to get adults to engage with Black history, Robin Walker 'The Black History Man,' is offering you the chance to learn more about Black or African contributions to history.

For this reason, The Black History Man is teaching a short course about Black people in the History of Science and Technology. The programme consists of six content laden seminars:

1. Ancient Egyptian Contributions to Science and Technology
2. Mysterious Sciences of the Great Pyramid
3. West African Contributions to Science and Technology
4. Intellectual Life and Legacy of Timbuktu
5. African American Pioneers of Invention
6. African American Pioneers of Science

For more details on this course or any other enquiries, send an email to historicalwalker@yahoo.com

Other E-Book Lecture Essays by Robin Walker AVAILABLE NOW

Robin Walker, *The Rise and Fall of Black Wall Street*. Amazon Kindle Publications, 2011

Robin Walker, *Intellectual Life and Legacy of Timbuktu*, Amazon Kindle Publications, 2011

Robin Walker, *If You Want to Learn Early African History, START HERE*, Amazon Kindle Publications, 2011

Robin Walker, *The Black Musical Tradition*, Amazon Kindle Publications, 2011

Robin Walker, *The Equinox and the Real Story behind Easter*, Amazon Kindle Publications, 2011

Robin Walker, *Black Economic Empowerment*, Amazon Kindle Publications, 2011

Robin Walker, *Understanding the Book of the Dead*, Amazon Kindle Publications, 2011

Robin Walker, *The Mysterious Sciences of the Great Pyramid*, Amazon Kindle Publications, 2011

Robin Walker, *West African Contributions to Sciences and Technology*, Amazon Kindle Publications, 2012

Robin Walker, *Ancient Egyptian Contributions to Science and Technology*, Amazon Kindle Publications, 2012

To purchase these Kindle e-books, find them through amazon.com or amazon.co.uk

SOURCES OF INFORMATION

Introduction: In the Space Sciences

Curtis M. Graves and Ivan Van Sertima, *Space Science: The African-American Contribution,* in Ivan Van Sertima ed, *Blacks in Science: Ancient and Modern,* US, Transaction Publishers, 1983, pp.238-257

James G. Spady, *Blackspace,* in Ivan Van Sertima ed, *Blacks in Science: Ancient and Modern,* US, Transaction Publishers, 1983, pp.258-262

Samuel Kennedy Yeboah, *The Ideology of Racism,* UK, Hansib Publishing, 1997, pp.201-204 and 222

Various Wikipedia and Internet pages

Chapter 1: Early African American Pioneers of Science

Hunter Havelin Adams III, *African & African-American Contributions to Science and Technology,* US, Portland Public Schools, 1987, pp.68-69 and 74

Henry E. Baker, *Benjamin Banneker, the Negro Mathematician and Astronomer,* see http://www.jstor.org/stable/2713484?seq=14

Louis Haber, *Black Pioneers of Science and Invention,* US, Harcourt, Brace, Jovanovich, 1971, pp.1-19

Ivan Van Sertima, *African Smallpox Inoculation Introduced into Early Eighteenth-Century America,* in Ivan Van Sertima ed, *Egypt: Child of Africa,* US, Transaction Publishers, 1994, p.269

Theodore Walker Jr., *The Liberating Role of Astronomy in an Old Farmer's Almanac: David Rittenhouse's "Useful Knowledge" and a Benjamin Banneker Almanac for 1792*
see http://journalofcosmology.com/JOC19/walker4a.cor3.pdf

Various Wikipedia and Internet pages

Chapter 2: African American Pioneers in Invention

Hunter Havelin Adams III, *African & African-American Contributions to Science and Technology*, US, Portland Public Schools, 1987, pp.71-79

Henry E. Baker, *The Colored Inventor: A Record of Fifty Years*, US, The Crisis Publishing Company, 1913, pp.10-11

John Henrik Clarke, *Lewis Latimer - Bringer of the Light*, in Ivan Van Sertima ed, *Blacks in Science: Ancient and Modern*, US, Transaction Publishers, 1983, pp.229-237

Louis Haber, *Black Pioneers of Science and Invention*, US, Harcourt, Brace, Jovanovich, 1971, pp.20-103

Robert C. Hayden, *Black Americans in the field of Science and Invention*, in Ivan Van Sertima ed, *Blacks in Science: Ancient and Modern*, US, Transaction Publishers, 1983, pp.215-228

J. A. Rogers, *World's Great Men of Color, Volume 2*, US, Macmillan, 1972, pp.352-354

Samuel Kennedy Yeboah, *The Ideology of Racism*, UK, Hansib Publishing, 1997, pp.185-195 and 199-201

Various Wikipedia and Internet pages

Chapter 3: African American Pioneers in Mathematics and Physics

Hunter Havelin Adams III, *African & African-American Contributions to Science and Technology*, US, Portland Public Schools, 1987, pp.78-79

Beatrice Lumpkin, *African & African-American Contributions to Mathematics*, US, Portland Public Schools, 1987, p.43

John Pappademos, *An Outline of Africa's Role in the History of Physics*, in Ivan Van Sertima ed, *Blacks in Science: Ancient and Modern*, US, Transaction Publishers, 1983, pp.192-193

James G. Spady, *Blackspace,* in Ivan Van Sertima ed, *Blacks in Science: Ancient and Modern,* US, Transaction Publishers, 1983, pp.262-263

Samuel Kennedy Yeboah, *The Ideology of Racism,* UK, Hansib Publishing, 1997, pp.220, 221

Various Wikipedia and Internet pages

Chapter 4: African American Pioneers in Biology, Botany and Zoology

Louis Haber, *Black Pioneers of Science and Invention,* US, Harcourt, Brace, Jovanovich, 1971, pp.104-121, 161-175

J. A. Rogers, *World's Great Men of Color, Volume 2,* US, Macmillan, 1972, pp.443-447 and 462-473

Samuel Kennedy Yeboah, *The Ideology of Racism,* UK, Hansib Publishing, 1997, pp.204-220

Various Wikipedia and Internet pages

Chapter 5: African American Pioneers in Chemistry

Louis Haber, *Black Pioneers of Science and Invention,* US, Harcourt, Brace, Jovanovich, 1971, pp.122-160

J. A. Rogers, *World's Great Men of Color, Volume 2,* US, Macmillan, 1972, p.561

Ivan Van Sertima, *African-American Scientists Played Major Role in Atomic Bomb Development,* in Ivan Van Sertima ed, *Egypt: Child of Africa,* US, Transaction Publishers, 1994, pp.270-272

Ivan Van Sertima, *Dr Lloyd Quarterman - Nuclear Scientist,* in Ivan Van Sertima ed, *Blacks in Science: Ancient and Modern,* US, Transaction Publishers, 1983, pp.266-272

Samuel Kennedy Yeboah, *The Ideology of Racism,* UK, Hansib Publishing, 1997, pp.198, 220-221

Various Wikipedia and Internet pages

Chapter 6: African American Pioneers in Medicine and Surgery

Louis Haber, *Black Pioneers of Science and Invention,* US, Harcourt, Brace, Jovanovich, 1971, pp.176-200, 219-244

Carl Murphy, *Maryland Adopts Colored Physician Syphilis Test as State's Standard,* in *The Afro American,* 31 October 1942, p.1

J. A. Rogers, *World's Great Men of Color, Volume 2,* US, Macmillan, 1972, pp.561 and 563

Samuel Kennedy Yeboah, *The Ideology of Racism,* UK, Hansib Publishing, 1997, pp.195-198

Various Wikipedia and Internet pages

INDEX

Blacks and Science
Volume One

Ancient Egyptian Contributions to Science and Technology

AND

The Mysterious Sciences of the Great Pyramid

Robin Walker

CPSIA information can be obtained at www.ICGtesting.com
Printed in the USA
LVOW10s1039220116

471868LV00023B/680/P